TH EASY W TREE RECOGNITION

JOHN KILBRACKEN

KINGFISHER BOOKS

For Sue

Kingfisher Books, Grisewood & Dempsey Ltd,
Elsley House, 24–30 Great Titchfield Street,
London W1P 7AD

This edition first published in 1989 by Kingfisher Books

Originally published in hardcover in 1983

BRITISH LIBRARY CATALOGUING IN PUBLICATION DATA
Kilbracken, John Godley, *Baron, 1920–*
The easy way to tree recognition
1. Great Britain. Trees
I. Title
582.160941
ISBN 0 86272 398 1

Design by Adrian Hodgkins
Illustrations by Norma Birgin and Terry Callcut
Photographs by the author
Phototypeset by Southern Positives and Negatives (SPAN),
Lingfield, Surrey
Printed in Italy by Vallardi Industrie Grafiche, Milan

How to Use this Book

This book has only one purpose – to help you to identify, as quickly and easily as possible, the trees most likely to be seen in Britain and Ireland. It is thus a companion volume to my previous book, *The Easy Way to Bird Recognition*, and I have used exactly the same method.

There are already many excellent books on trees, but none of them is designed solely to assist beginners with identification. Instead you find you have to work through the book looking at the pictures, till you hit on what seems to be the right tree.

The Easy Way to Tree Recognition, like its predecessor, provides a method that is very much simpler and leads you to the correct identification much more quickly and directly by means of a systematic key. If you glance through it, you will see that the key consists of a series of intermingled Questions and Answers, numbered consecutively from 1 to 172. The Questions are numbered in green, the Answers in orange.

When you wish to identify a tree, you always start off by turning to Question 1. Have a look at it now. You'll see that it asks you if the tree's leaves are needle-like. Probably you will know already what is meant by "needle-like". If you don't, or if in this particular case you are not quite sure of the right answer, the drawings and text accompanying the Question will make it easy for you to decide. You are then instructed to turn to Question 2 if you decide that the answer is 'Yes' – i.e. that the leaves are in fact needle-like – or to Question 43 if you decide that it is 'No'. In either case, you then find yourself asked about some other feature of the tree and are given similar guidance. Your reply leads you to a third Question.

In this way you are led easily, rather as though you were following the clues on a treasure hunt, onwards through the book; and all the time you know you are coming closer to identification. You will seldom have any doubts about your replies because, apart from the help given, each Question has been carefully chosen to make it as easy as possible. All obscure, technical language has been avoided, including such botanical terms as are unknown to most beginners, and any that are unavoidable are carefully explained.

After perhaps as few as three or four Questions, and never more than a dozen, you'll find you've arrived at the Answer. Almost always, each species has an Answer to itself – much more often than in my bird book – and your quest is at once over. Very occasionally, when two or three species are easily confused, they are grouped together in the same Answer so that the little differences between them may be indicated, and you should find it easy to choose between them.

In either case, the tree or trees are illustrated in colour on the same page, and the accompanying text sets out the basic details of each species. As a general rule, these are confined to facts that might help you to recognize the tree, but other information of special interest may be included, and the maximum height attained by trees of the species is always given.

Now let's follow a series of questions through to show how the book works. Let's suppose you wish to identify one particular pine tree. You have often before seen trees of this species but do not know its name. Starting at Question 1, you at once see that its leaves ARE needle-like, so you turn to Question 2. Here you find you are asked if the needles grow singly: you discover on examining them, perhaps to your surprise, that they do NOT, but always emerge from a sheath IN PAIRS. You therefore turn, as directed, to Question 29 and from there to Question 30 which asks you about the length of the needles. Obviously some of the needles are longer than others, but here you have little difficulty in deciding that these ones are LESS THAN TEN CENTIMETRES. You are directed to Question 31 and thence to 33, which you at once see is your Answer. A glance at the illustrations and at the accompanying text convinces you that the tree is in fact a Scots Pine.

On the author's land at Killegar in Ireland, century-old beech turn golden brown in autumn.

When you get to know the book and become more experienced (or perhaps you are experienced enough already) so that you need no help with the Questions, it will be more convenient to use the abbreviated key at the very end of the book, just before the indexes, which will lead you much more quickly towards your Answer.

If the tree you are looking up does not agree with the illustrations or description, there are only two possible explanations. Either you have made a mistake, and should go back to the beginning to make absolutely sure that all your replies have been correct, or you have come across a species of tree too seldom seen for inclusion in this book.

Deciding which species to include was much more difficult with trees than it was with birds, which are all truly wild. Many of them are so rarely seen – and then are often so shy and elusive, or inhabit such remote areas – that they are extremely unlikely to be seen by a beginner and could safely be omitted.

With trees it's very different. Many species grow wild – by which I mean that they are self-sown – but much more often they have been planted. And there is nothing to stop people from trying their luck with any species, however rare, if they can get hold of a specimen. Indeed some people make a hobby of planting unusual trees. Even in the most built-up urban area, a specimen of a very rare species may have been planted in a front garden and lovingly nurtured till it is tree-sized. There is no difficulty in spotting such a tree, as there would be with an equally rare bird, but over 1000 species would have to be included, not to mention varieties and cultivars, if every tree that users of this book might come across were to be covered. Many books do include several hundred species, which is admirable but makes the books much harder for beginners to use to identify the common trees that will constitute the vast majority – perhaps all – of those they see.

I have therefore confined this book to those chosen as being the 114 commonest.

In some ways, trees are easier to identify than birds. First and foremost, they never fly away. You will never have to use this book after catching the briefest glimpse of a tree as it flitted through the undergrowth! It is standing there in front of you. You have all the time in the world to take note of every detail. If you have this book with you, you can identify it on the spot, making sure you have all the facts needed, taking measurements if necessary, to answer each of the Questions.

In other ways, trees are more difficult. All birds of the same species are usually more or less identical. Where substantial differences do occur – between the male and the female, or between summer and winter plumage, for example – these too are standardized.

But trees of the same species may vary greatly in appearance, depending on age, site, climate, or individual whim. For example, the bark of many species, such as the well-known oak and ash, is completely smooth when the tree is young. As it grows older, it begins to develop a few barely noticeable vertical fissures. These deepen and multiply till they are a very prominent feature.

The shape of trees, too, is extremely variable. For instance, a beech that is 'open grown', such as a single tree in the middle of a field, usually has a short, stubby trunk, quickly dividing into many huge, spreading branches which form an immense, semi-circular crown reaching almost to the ground. But a 'close grown' beech in dense woodland, with many other trees nearby, may have a perfectly straight trunk for many metres with few, if any, sizeable branches, and its crown will be quite small.

The flowers and fruit of trees are not liable to such variation, and in many species are so conspicuous that they would make recognition easy. Unfortunately, they are only present at certain times of the year – and individual trees may even decide not to flower at all. I planted a walnut 25 years ago and am still awaiting the first catkins.

In the end it is the leaves of trees that are the greatest help in distinguishing a species, though it is also true that leaves, even those on the same tree, may be very dissimilar. They may vary greatly in size. They usually change colour with the season (though this is often a help). And sometimes those on one part of a tree differ completely in shape from those on another. Nonetheless they are sufficiently consistent to provide by far the most important clues to identification, and I have relied on them very heavily.

This means, unfortunately, that this book cannot be used in winter months, except to identify evergreens. The identification of trees that are completely bare of foliage may often, in any case, be very difficult. But you will find, as you gain experience, having first learnt to distinguish the trees mainly by their leaves, that it is possible to tell what many of them are even when they are bare.

JK
Killegar
1983

Are all its leaves needle-like?

Some trees, all of them conifers, have the extremely narrow leaves probably already known to you as 'needles'. In this book, they are considered needle-like if they are less than 3mm wide *and* at least four times as long as they are wide.

The leaves of certain species are usually described as being 'awl-shaped'. Though relatively broad-based, curving quickly to a point, they fall within the above definition of 'needles'.

Answer 'Yes' if *all* the foliage is needle-like. Answer 'No' in all other cases, including those in which a few young leaves may be needles but not the great mass of foliage.

Note that each needle is in fact a separate leaf, though it may look more like part of one.

Yes 2   No 43

Awl-shaped leaves

NEEDLE-LIKE LEAVES

Do the needles grow singly?

2

(from 1)

Answer 'Yes' if each needle grows singly and independently from its own individual base along a central twig or shoot. Answer 'No' if at least two needles, and perhaps as many as 20 or even more, always emerge together from the same base.

Yes 3   No 29

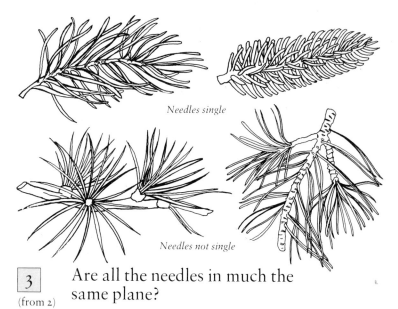

Needles single

Needles not single

3

(from 2)

Are all the needles in much the same plane?

Answer 'Yes' if the needles are all, or very nearly all, in much the same plane to right and left of their twig, arranged along it regularly to form a noticeably flattened, 'herring-bone' pattern. Choose 'No' if they grow round their twig in several quite different planes.

Yes 4   No 11

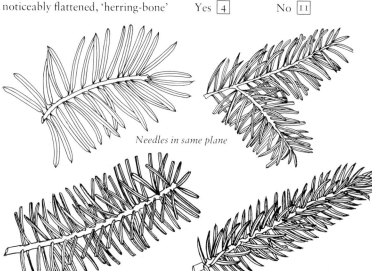

Needles in same plane

Needles in different planes

(from 3)

If it is deciduous, its leaves are light green and delicate till they turn reddish-brown in autumn and then all fall, so that the branches are bare in winter. Otherwise it is evergreen.

If in doubt, have a look at 5 before turning on to 6.

Deciduous [5]
Evergreen [6]

5   DAWN REDWOOD
(Metasequoia glyptostroboides)

(from 4)

Leaves turn brick-red in autumn

Young cones   *Autumn tree*   *Summer*

This is one of the few deciduous conifers and the only common one with needles that grow singly, making a very regular 'herring-bone' pattern, in opposite pairs along twigs, which are also in opposite pairs.

The rather small cones (18–25mm) hang from individual stalks about 5cm long. They are roundish or cylindrical, and turn from green to brown. Almost all the branches point slightly upward, so that the tree has a narrow outline. The bark is reddish- or orange-brown. In older trees it flakes off or peels, and the trunk becomes deeply fluted.

As a forest tree in its native China, this redwood reaches 35m, but has not yet exceeded 20m in Britain, where it is grown ornamentally.

6   Is the bark very soft and spongey?

(from 4)
Answer 'Yes' if the bark, which is
reddish-brown, is so soft that you
can punch it quite hard with your
clenched fish and it doesn't hurt.
Otherwise answer 'No'.

Yes [7]   No [8]

CALIFORNIA REDWOOD or Coast Redwood
(Sequoia sempervirens)
(from 6)

This redwood is the world's tallest
tree, having reached 112m in its
native California. In the British Isles
it seldom exceeds 40m.

  Its needles are very short
(6–20mm). They are arranged neatly
along each twig in flat regular ranks.
Small yellow or green flowers appear
as early as February. The cones
(20–30mm) grow singly at the very
tips of shoots; they ripen from green
to brown. The reddish-brown bark
becomes quite deeply fissured.

  The Wellingtonia is the only other
tree with a 'punchable' trunk but its
leaves are not all in much the same
plane (see 18).

All year

*Flat pointed needles
arranged in opposite
pairs*

*Mature
cone*

Does it have a very straight, undivided trunk?

Answer 'Yes' if the trunk of the tree rises straight and undivided for all its length, with side branches radiating at regular intervals from it. Answer 'No' if the main trunk is rather short, and very soon divides into two or more separate stems, so that the tree is rather bushy in appearance.

Yes 9   No 10

9
(from 8)

GRAND FIR or Giant Fir
(Abies grandis)

On some sites, this large forest tree grows faster than any other. It reaches 50m and is often planted commercially.

Its flat needles, up to 5cm long, grow in regular ranks along each side of their twigs. They have notched tips and are rather irregular in length. The cones are cylindrical and quite large (5–10cm); they turn from green to brown.

The bark is greenish-grey or brownish-grey. It is often covered with resinous blisters and becomes darker with age.

All year

Mature cone shows no bracts

Needles parted in flat spray

COMMON YEW or English Yew
(Taxus baccata)

All year

*Reddish-brown bark
peels off in
vertical flakes*

*Red, fleshy
cup-shaped
fruit*

*Dark-green
sharp-pointed
needles*

The yew seldom grows tall, though exceptional specimens, perhaps over 1000 years old, may sometimes reach 20m. The usually furrowed trunk, which has reddish-brown bark with a tendency to flake, almost always divides into separate stems.

The yew's fruit is easily distinguished from any other conifer's. It ripens from an inconspicuous green flower to resemble a red berry of very distinctive shape. The flat, dark green needles have quite sharp points. They grow regularly along their twigs in two distinct, flattened rows, forming a regular pattern. Their undersides are paler. Often grown in graveyards.

Several different varieties of yew have been developed. Much the commonest is the Irish yew (*Taxus baccata* 'Fastigiata'), which has distinctive twisted needles and many leaders (see illustration).

*Irish Yew,
distinguished
by its many
leaders*

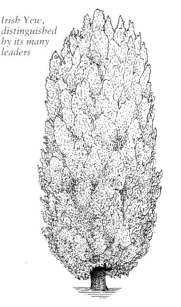

How do its needles grow?

(from 3)

Turn to 12 if, on very careful examination, you find that each needle grows from its twig on a very small, woody 'peg' – a characteristic of the spruces. The peg remains behind on the twig when the needle falls.

Choose 15 if the needles are short (about 10mm) and grow in regular whorls of three, at inter·als along their twig. Otherwise, go on to 16.

From small woody pegs 12
In whorls of three 15
Neither of these 16

Needles in whorls of 3

12   What colour are its needles?

(from 11)

The two best-known spruces are most easily distinguished because the sitka's needles have blue-grey undersides; they are very strong and prickly, reaching 30mm in length. Those of the Norway are much the same colour above and below – a rather lighter green. They are softer and do not exceed 20mm. Choose your answer accordingly.

Blue-grey undersides 13
All green 14

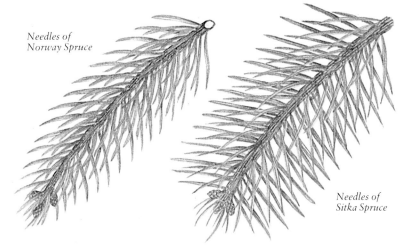

Needles of Norway Spruce

Needles of Sitka Spruce

SITKA SPRUCE or Silver Spruce
(Picea sitchensis)

This very fast growing tree is the one most widely planted commercially. It often grows a metre in a year, reaching a height of 80m in its area of origin (North America) and 50m in Britain.

The blue-grey tinge of its needles (1–3cm), which are vigorous and prickly, is its most distinctive feature. Its flowers – both male and female – are cone-like and quite large (up to 4cm). They usually open in May. The cones (6–10cm) hang downwards; they ripen from green to brown. Their scales are paper-thin and have crinkly edges.

The bark of young trees is dark grey and rather smooth, later becoming flecked with purple and flaking.

Mature cone with crinkly-edged scales

All year

Blue-green, long, thin and sharp needles

NORWAY SPRUCE
(Picea abies)

(from 12)

This is the species almost always used for Christmas trees, so it is well known to nearly everyone.

Its needles (1–2cm) grow regularly along each twig, mostly to right and left of it (more so than the sitka spruce – see 13) but also from its upper and, less often, from its lower surface. The hanging cones are noticeably large (12–18cm) and are often numerous, even on young trees. The bark, reddish-brown and smooth at first, darkens. Later it may flake into irregular, circular scales.

If intended as Christmas trees, Norway spruces are planted closer together, and usually harvested when they reach 1–3m. But they are also very widely grown for their timber and reach over 40m.

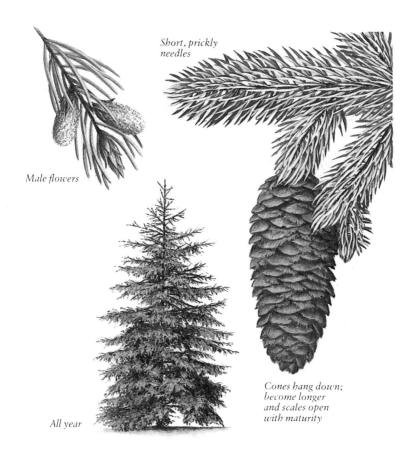

Short, prickly needles

Male flowers

All year

Cones hang down; become longer and scales open with maturity

COMMON JUNIPER
(Juniperus communis)

Only the common juniper has its needles in whorls of three. Very variable in shape, it is often shrub-like in appearance with several separate stems, but some specimens become true trees, occasionally elongated, and may reach 8m. The needles (10–15mm) are pointed and delicate. Their upper sides are green, with a pale central band; they are grey-green below. The bark is usually reddish-brown.

The male cones are very inconspicuous. The female cones, which always grow on separate trees; look like smooth round berries (6–10mm). They ripen from green to blue to black, and are used for flavouring gin.

All year

Ripe berry-like cones

16   Are the leaves awl-shaped?

(from 11)
Answer 'Yes' if the needle-like leaves, though relatively broad-based, curve quickly to a point. Answer 'No' if their margins are parallel, or nearly so, for their whole length.

Yes 17   No 20

What length are the leaves?

(from 16)
This question needs no elaboration.

Not more than 7mm |18|
About 15mm |19|

18 WELLINGTONIA or Giant Sequoia or California Big Tree
(Sequoiadendron giganteum)

(from 17)

The awl-shaped leaves of the Wellingtonia grow in spirals around their twigs, completely hiding them. They are blue-grey at first, later becoming dark green.

   The reddish-brown bark of these magnificent trees is perhaps their most distinctive feature. It is so soft and spongey that, as with the California redwood (see 7), you can punch it with your clenched fist and it doesn't hurt.

   Wellingtonias in California are usually close grown and therefore have long clean trunks. One of them is the largest (but not the tallest) tree in the world, weighing over 1000 tonnes. In Britain they are almost always specimen trees, growing alone or in avenues, so they are usually conical with branches quite close to the ground. They have exceeded 50m in height.

   The oval cones are of average size (5–8cm).

All year

Awl-shaped leaves grow in spirals away from twig

Mature cone; corky with grooved scales

JAPANESE CEDAR or Japanese Red Cedar
(Cryptomeria japonica)

(from 17)

This species and its many varieties (which are not included here) is frequently grown ornamentally in parks and gardens, sometimes in towns.

Its awl-shaped leaves grow spirally around their twigs, curving in towards them. They may turn bronze in winter. This cedar has quite distinctive cones. They are very small (15–20mm) and rounded, each with 20–30 hooked scales. These make the cones irregular in appearance as they ripen from green to brown.

The bark is soft and fissured. The tree usually has a regular, conical shape and may reach 35m.

Long awl-like needles

Mature cone, round with hooks on scales

All year

Soft, fissured bark peels off in long strips

20 Does it have large, erect cones?

(from 16)

Answer 'Yes' if the cones are very large (at least 12cm) and grow vertically upwards. Answer 'No' if they hang downwards and do not exceed 8cm. If no cones are to be seen, have a look at 21–28 to discover other distinguishing features.

Yes 21   No 24

Cone large and upright

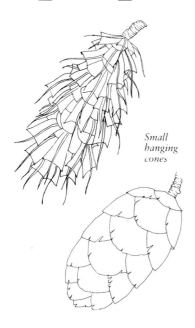

Small hanging cones

21 Do the needles curve upwards?

(from 20)

Answer 'Yes' if most of the needles, after leaving their twig more or less horizontally, make a right angle to curve almost vertically upwards, almost hiding the twig. Answer 'No' if they are nearly straight, forming something like a herring-bone pattern, so that the whole twig is easily visible.

Yes 22   No 23

The noble fir is best distinguished by its densely-growing, blue-tinged needles (10–35mm), which are flat with rounded tips and mostly curve steeply upwards from their shoot.

Even more distinctive are its enormous cones (12–25cm), but they grow only from the very topmost branches and are seldom seen unless the tree is young. They are erect, roughly cylindrical and nearly half as broad as they are long. When they are ripe, they break up to release the seeds, leaving a bare vertical spike. The branches of the noble fir usually grow horizontally to form a regular pattern.

This is a fast-growing species and reaches a height of 45m – even more in its native North America. In Britain it is often grown ornamentally, but is also planted for its timber.

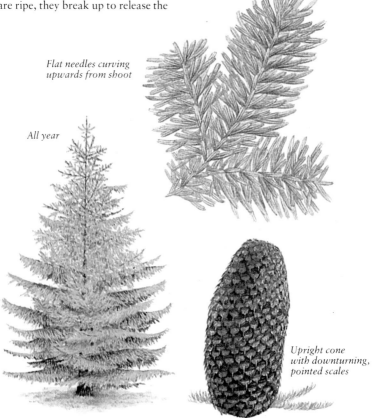

Flat needles curving upwards from shoot

All year

Upright cone with downturning, pointed scales

SILVER FIR
(Abies alba)

Once widely grown for its timber, this species is now quite seldom planted. Most trees to be seen are probably over a century old. They reach 50m.

The silver fir's large cones (12–18cm) are usually conspicuous, but eventually they shed their scales, leaving a bare vertical spike. Each scale has a noticeable bract, which turns downward towards the base of the cone. The needles (up to 25mm) are flattened and quite dark green.

Most grow in much the same plane to right and left of their twig in a regular herring-bone pattern, but others, which are shorter, grow upwards from its top surface.

The bark is grey or silver-grey, smooth in young trees, but becoming cracked and ridged with age. The silver fir, when open grown, has more of a tendency than most other conifers to develop two or more separate trunks, often with large side branches.

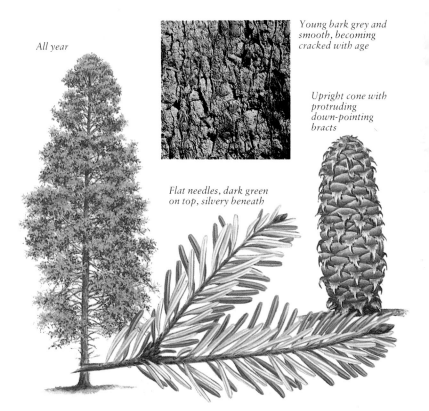

All year

Young bark grey and smooth, becoming cracked with age

Upright cone with protruding down-pointing bracts

Flat needles, dark green on top, silvery beneath

Do the needles have sharp tips?

(from 20)

Answer 'Yes' if the tips of the needles are pointed. Answer 'No' if they are rounded.

Yes 25   No 26

25 **DOUGLAS FIR**
(Pseudotsuga menziesii)

(from 24)

The cones of the Douglas fir, which turn from green to brown, are surprisingly small for such a large forest tree (5–8cm). They have feathery, 3-pointed bracts turning downwards – a unique feature. Its needles (2–3cm) grow all around their twig, but mostly to each side of it, forming dense foliage. They are aromatic. If you detach one of them, it leaves an oval scar on the stalk.

The bark of young trees is smooth and grey, sometimes with resinous blisters. Later it becomes reddish-brown or purplish, and is cork-like with many ridges and fissures.

The Douglas fir is widely planted for its fine timber and reaches 60m. It is the tallest tree now growing in Britain.

Female tassel-like flowers

All year

Male flowers

Flat, pointed needles grow all round twig

Oval cone with feathery 3-pointed bracts

(from 24)

Answer 'Yes' if the tree grows with a single stem or trunk, which rises undivided all the way from the ground. Answer 'No' if the main trunk divides close to the ground into at least two separate stems and often more.

Yes 27   No 28

27   WESTERN HEMLOCK
(*Tsuga heterophylla*)

(from 26)

The Western hemlock's most noticeable feature is its very delicate leader – the name given to the topmost shoot of a tree. It droops to such an extent that it is often pointing almost vertically downward, especially in young trees. The needles often vary noticeably in length from their neighbours, ranging in size from 10 to 20mm. Flattened with rounded tips, they are dark green above and grey-green below. The cones are quite small (20–30mm). Green and oval when unripe, they open up later to become scaly as they turn brown.

This fast-growing species is often planted commercially. It reaches 35m and is specially useful because it tolerates deep shade and can therefore be used for underplanting.

Fissured, sometimes flaky, bark

Leader

All year

Flat, sharp needles vary in length

Young cone; scales open with maturity

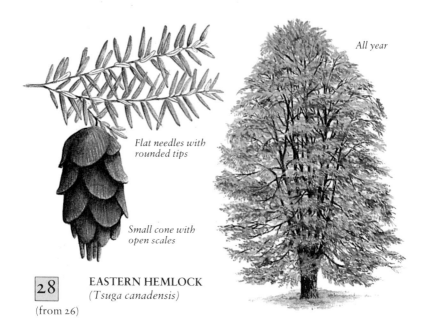

All year

Flat needles with rounded tips

Small cone with open scales

28 EASTERN HEMLOCK
(Tsuga canadensis)

(from 26)

In its native Canada, the Eastern hemlock grows straight and true, which makes it suitable for timber, but in Britain it has developed an almost invariable tendency to fork close to the ground and it is never grown commercially. The lower branches often droop down to the ground or close to it. The short needles (up to 15mm) are quite regular in length, noticeably tapered, with rounded tips. Their undersides have two parallel silver bands, which make them almost white-looking. The cones are like those of the Western hemlock (see 27) but smaller (20mm). They grow, almost always, at the very end of their twigs.

In Britain this species seldom exceeds 20m in height, but may occasionally reach 30m.

29 How many needles emerge together from the same base?

(from 2)

You have decided that the needles do not grow singly. Now consider how many needles emerge together from the same sheath at their base. If they are in pairs, threes or fives, it is certain to be a pine and you should choose your next Question accordingly. If they are in bunches of ten or more – perhaps as many as twenty – it is either a larch or a cedar and you should go on to 40.

Two 30
Three 36
Five 37
Ten or more 40

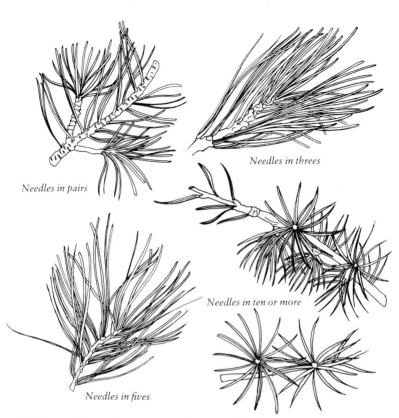

Needles in pairs

Needles in threes

Needles in ten or more

Needles in fives

30   How long are the needles?

(from 29)

Turn to 31 if virtually all the needles are less than 10cm in length, and to 34 if their average length is about 15cm. Choose 35 if the needles are very strong with rough edges, and grow to 25cm.

Less than 10cm [31]
About 15cm [34]
Up to 25cm [35]

31   Are the cones quite small (less than 5cm)?

(from 30)

Answer 'Yes' if the cones have small prickles and do not exceed 5cm in length. Answer 'No' if they have smooth scales and are 6–8cm long. If no cones are visible, have a look at 32 before turning on to 33.

Yes [32]   No [33]

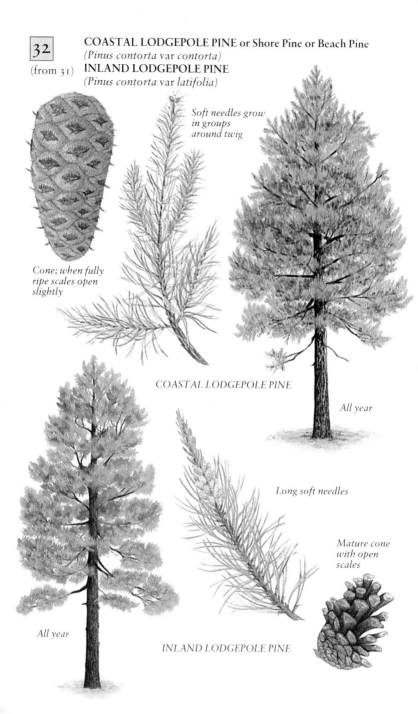

(from 31)

32 **COASTAL LODGEPOLE PINE** or Shore Pine or Beach Pine
(Pinus contorta var *contorta)*
INLAND LODGEPOLE PINE
(Pinus contorta var *latifolia)*

Soft needles grow in groups around twig

Cone; when fully ripe scales open slightly

COASTAL LODGEPOLE PINE

All year

Long soft needles

Mature cone with open scales

All year

INLAND LODGEPOLE PINE

These two varieties of the lodgepole pine are quite similar and it is convenient to consider them together. Despite their names, neither is particularly associated in Britain with coastal or inland regions.

The main difference is that the so-called coastal variety has shorter needles (up to 5cm) than the other's (up to 10cm); also they grow more densely and are more of a yellowish green. The cones of both are similar. They usually grow in pairs, up to 5cm in length, and are egg-shaped; they ripen in two years, but may not fall for many years.

Both varieties are useful forest trees because they tolerate poor soil. The coastal lodgepole pine is the more commonly planted, though it grows less tall (up to 25m) than the more slender inland variety (up to 35m).

33 SCOTS PINE
(Pinus sylvestris)
(from 31)

This is the only native pine – and much the commonest. It is most easily distinguished from other pines by its shorter needles (not more than 7cm). The oval cones (up to 8cm) grow singly and take three years to ripen. At first they are green and egg-shaped. Later they become rounder as they open up and turn brown.

When it is a young tree, the branches of the Scots pine grow in regular radiations to form the conical shape typical of most conifers. As the tree grows older, the bark becomes reddish-brown and is also increasingly fissured. But it tends to flake away from the upper trunk and branches, which become quite smooth with an unmistakable orange-brown tinge. The lower branches begin to die and fall, till a mature tree is often almost branchless for almost all its length, with a small rounded crown. This species will tolerate poor soil and is often planted commercially. It reaches 35m.

All year

Mature cone

Long, stiff needles grow in pairs

CORSICAN PINE
(Pinus nigra var *maritima)*
AUSTRIAN PINE
(Pinus nigra var *nigra)*

These two varieties of *Pinus nigra* are very similar and best considered together. The Corsican is much the commoner.

Both have long needles (up to 18cm), growing densely in forward-pointing pairs. Those of the Corsican, which are often twisted, are less coarse and sharp than the

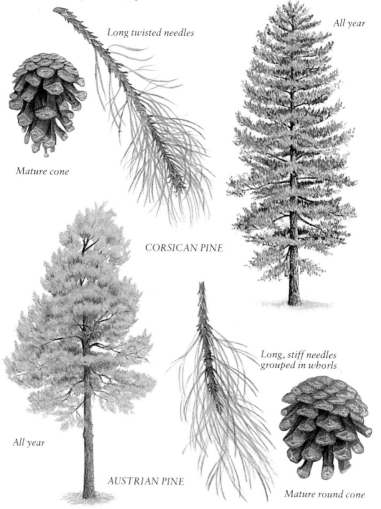

Long twisted needles

Mature cone

All year

CORSICAN PINE

All year

Long, stiff needles grouped in whorls

AUSTRIAN PINE

Mature round cone

Austrian's. The former's buds (2cm) are twice the length of the latter's but come to a less sharp point. The two trees have almost identical cones. Up to 8cm in length, they are at first green and egg-shaped, becoming rounder as they ripen and turn brown.

Both varieties reach about 35m and are often planted as windbreaks in coastal regions, usually on sandy ground. The Austrian pine, unlike the Corsican, has a tendency to develop two or more trunks as it grows older. This makes it less suitable for timber, for which the single-stemmed Corsican pine is quite widely grown.

35 MARITIME PINE
(Pinus pinaster)

(from 30)

This is the last of the 2-needle pines included in this book. It is at once identified by its very long needles (up to 25cm). Stouter than those of any other pine, they have rough edges and come to a sharp point. The cones (up to 20cm) usually grow downwards in pairs or threes. Roughly egg-shaped, they ripen from green to brown, and usually stay on the tree for many years before falling.

As its name indicates, the maritime pine is most at home by the sea, often as a windbreak on sand dunes. In Britain it is seldom seen except on the south coast. The bark has vertical fissures and is often reddish brown or purplish. In older trees, which may reach 33m, the lower branches die off, leaving a long bare trunk and an often rounded crown.

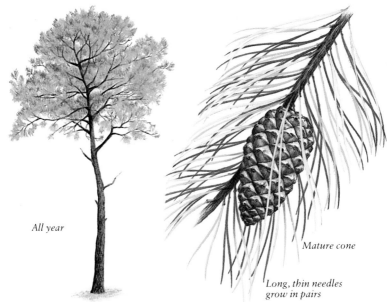

All year

Mature cone

Long, thin needles grow in pairs

MONTEREY PINE
(Pinus radiata)

The needles of the Monterey pine are distinctive because, among those of pines commonly seen, they alone grow in threes from the same base. They are also very long (10–15cm). The extremely hard cones are egg-shaped but tend to be lop-sided. Very variable in length (7–15cm), they often grow in bunches and stay unopened on the branches. The bark is usually grey, but may also be dark brown. It becomes quite deeply fissured.

This species reaches 30m and is usually planted to form windbreaks or for ornament. Its wind resistance makes it specially suitable for exposed sites, often on the coast.

All year

Mature lop-sided cone

Long needles grow in threes

Does it have delicate, blue-tinged needles?

Of the two 5-needle pines included in this book, one has delicate, slender needles with a noticeable blueish tinge. If you can see any cones, they are pointed and quite long (up to 15cm). Answer 'Yes' and turn to 38.

The other's needles grow more densely; they are rigid, may be very finely toothed, and are dark green above, silver-green below. The cones are much smaller (up to 8cm) and rounded rather than pointed. Answer 'No' and turn to 39.

Yes 38   No 39

All year

WEYMOUTH PINE

Soft needles grow in fives

Mature cone with open scales

All year

AROLLA PINE

Dense, long needles
grow in fives

Mature cone;
pointed open scales

38	**WEYMOUTH PINE**

(Pinus strobus)

(from 37)

The main differences between the
two 5-needle pines have already been
noted (see 37).

The bark of the Weymouth pine is
smooth when the tree is young; it
becomes fissured with age and the
lower branches tend to die and fall.
At the same time, the crown develops
from being roughly conical to flat-
topped. May reach 30m.

39	**AROLLA PINE** or Swiss stone pine

(Pinus cembra)

(from 37)

The main differences between the
two 5-needle pines have already been
noted (see 37).

The Arolla pine usually keeps
most of its lower branches and
remains conical in shape, sometimes
reaching 25m. The undersides of the
needles are noticeably whitish.

Is it deciduous or evergreen?

(from 29)

Deciduous trees are those which lose all their foliage in winter. Turn to 41 if the delicate needles are a brilliant light green when they first appear in springtime, hardly darkening in summer till they turn yellow or orange-brown in autumn before falling. Choose 42 if the needles are less delicate and stay the same dark green all year, except for young leaves.

Deciduous 41
Evergreen 42

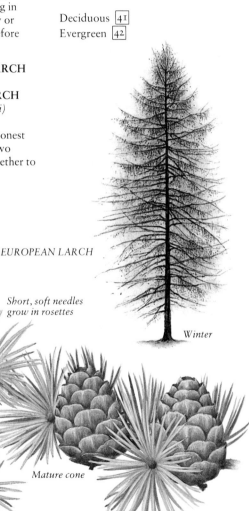

41 EUROPEAN LARCH
(Larix decidua)
(from 40) **JAPANESE LARCH**
(Larix kaempferi)

Larches are much the commonest deciduous conifers. These two similar species are taken together to help distinguish them.

EUROPEAN LARCH

Short, soft needles grow in rosettes

Winter

Female flowers

Mature cone

They are among the very first trees to burst into leaf in springtime, with vivid emerald foliage. Their needles. grow in clusters of 10–20 or more, with each cluster springing from the same sheath at its base.

The two species are not easy to tell apart except when they are in bloom. The female flowers of the European larch are unmistakable, being bright pink and cone-like. The other's are also cone-like but green or creamy yellow. The male flowers of both species are much less noticeable. They are smaller and less easy to tell apart: in both, they are globular and yellow.

The cones of the European larch are roughly egg-shaped and have smooth, regular scales. Those of the Japanese larch are rounder and the tops of their scales turn outward. In both cases they are unusually small (3–4cm). The needles of both are similar but the latter's tend to be rather broader (about 1mm), longer (about 4cm) and may have a blue-grey tinge.

In suitable sites, larches grow straight and true, with regular branches and a straight stem like most conifers, but sometimes the main trunk twists wildly or the branches head unpredictably upwards and downwards in all directions. Both species are planted widely for their timber and on suitable sites grow rapidly to exceed 30m. A natural cross between them, the hybrid larch *(Larix × eurolepsis)*, is sometimes planted.

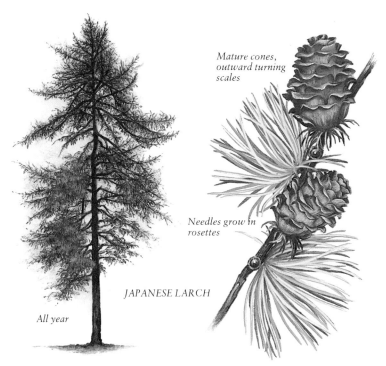

Mature cones, outward turning scales

Needles grow in rosettes

JAPANESE LARCH

All year

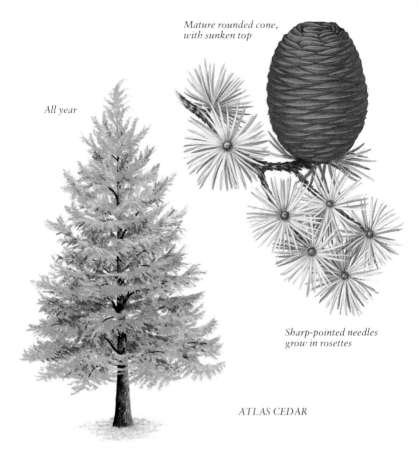

Mature rounded cone, with sunken top

All year

Sharp-pointed needles grow in rosettes

ATLAS CEDAR

42
(from 40)

ATLAS CEDAR or Atlantic Cedar
(Cedrus atlantica)
DEODAR or Himalayan Cedar
(Cedrus deodara)
CEDAR OF LEBANON
(Cedrus libani)

Cedars are the only evergreens likely to be seen with needles in bunches of at least ten (often far more), all rising from the same base. These three similar members of the genus – the only ones to grow commonly in the British Isles – are taken together to help distinguish them. This can usually be done best by noticing the general direction taken by the tips of their branches, and remembering those of the Atlas cedar tend to Ascend, of the Deodar to Descend and of the Lebanon cedar to be Level.

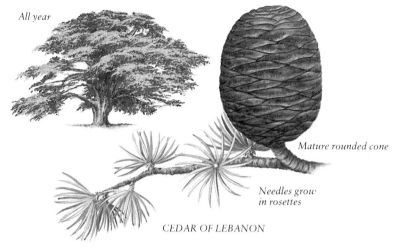

All year

Mature rounded cone

Needles grow in rosettes

CEDAR OF LEBANON

The deodar has the longest needles (up to 5cm), which grow in tufts of about a dozen. Those of the other two species are 2–3cm. The cedar of Lebanon's are in tufts of 10–20, the Atlas cedar's of 30–45. In all three species, the cones are quite large and rather egg-shaped, though the Atlas cedar's – which are much the smallest (5–8cm) – have hollowed tips. Those of the two others reach 14cm. All are bright green at first, turning brown as they ripen, and then breaking open to release the seeds. Cedars are peculiar in having noticeable male flowers looking very much like cones. The deodar's reach 12cm, more than twice the length of the others'.

The cedar of Lebanon tends to become flat-topped, while the two others usually remain conical. All three are nearly always grown ornamentally in the British Isles. They reach 35–40m.

DEODAR

All year

Needles in dense rosettes

Mature cone

Are its leaves in the form of scales?

(from 1)

Some trees – all evergreens – have most of their leaves, if not all, in the form of tiny scales, growing densely around their twigs and completely hiding them. They are so extremely small – never more than a mere 2–3mm in length – that beginners may not realize each is in fact a separate leaf. The foliage in general is often rather fern-like or cord-like.

Answer 'Yes' if your tree is one of these. Otherwise answer 'No'. The illustrations should make your choice quite easy. Note that some species have scale-like foliage except for their young leaves, which are needle-like. For these, turn to 45.

Yes 44   No 51

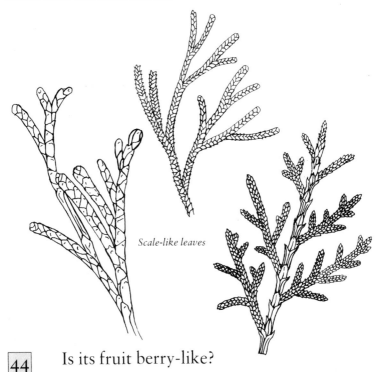

Scale-like leaves

44   Is its fruit berry-like?

(from 43)

Answer 'Yes' if the fruits are very small (under 6mm), and round or oval with smooth sides, so that they look more like berries than cones. Answer 'No' if they are orthodox,

woody cones and much larger (well over 6mm). If none is visible, have a look at 44 before turning on to 45.

Yes 45   No 46

45

(from 44)

CHINESE JUNIPER
(*Juniperus chinensis*)
PENCIL CEDAR or Red Cedar
(*Juniperus virginiana*)

As its scientific name shows, the pencil cedar is not a true cedar but a juniper. Hence its very small, berry-like cones (about 5mm), which are blue and egg-shaped. Those of the Chinese juniper are slightly larger, paler blue and irregularly spherical. The young leaves of both species are needle-like, growing in groups of 2 or 3, up to 6mm in the case of the pencil cedar and to twice that length in the Chinese juniper. The older, scale-like leaves are extremely small (less than 2mm), making the foliage cord-like. Those of the Chinese species are dark green, edged with light green, and rather blunt. The pencil cedar's are pointed and do not have light margins.

In the British Isles both trees are grown ornamentally and may reach 14–18m. Many cultivars of both species have been developed, generally similar but too numerous to include here.

Mature fruit

Scale-like leaves

All year

PENCIL CEDAR

All year

CHINESE JUNIPER

Immature fruits

Young leaves needle-like; older leaves scale-like

46   What size are the cones?

(from 44)

This question should be straight-
forward if cones are visible. If they
aren't, glance in turn at Answers
48–50 to make your choice.

10mm or less [47]
Over 20mm [50]

Spherical cone

47   Are the cones more or less spherical?

(from 46)

The illustrations will help you to
decide.

Yes [48] No [49]

Cone not spherical

Leader

48   LAWSON CYPRESS
(Chamaecyparis lawsoniana)

(from 47)

Scale-like leaves

All cypresses have more or less
spherical cones but, of the species
included here, only the Lawson
cypress has such small ones (less than
8mm). They are green and leathery at
first, opening up later to become
brown and woody. The leader of the
Lawson cypress invariably droops
downward – a very distinctive
feature – as do the tips of its
branches. Each scale-like leaf is
extremely small (about 2mm). They
grow in opposite pairs, completely
covering their twig. Each spray of
foliage is flattened and fern-like. The
bark is usually reddish-brown,
sometimes becoming purplish.

Mature open cone

Young cone

All year

    The Lawson cypress, reaching a
height of 35m, is perhaps the
commonest of all the conifers
planted for ornament. Many
cultivars have been developed,
varying greatly in shape and colour,
several of which do not have
drooping leaders.

49

WESTERN RED CEDAR
(Thuja plicata)
(from 47) **WHITE CEDAR**
(Thuja occidentalis)

These two species, which are not true cedars, are so similar that it is best to consider them together.

The cones of the western red cedar (about 10mm) have rounded scales with a small hook. Those of the white cedar are the same size but pointed.

The western red cedar grows to a greater height (40m) and is planted commercially. The white cedar does not exceed 20m in the British Isles, where it is only grown for ornament. The foliage of the western red cedar smells of resin when crushed, the white cedar's of apples. The latter has more of a tendency to have upswept branches and a divided trunk.

Scale-like leaves

Mature, open cone

All year

All year

WHITE CEDAR

All year

Scale-like leaves cover shoot

Mature cone

WESTERN RED CEDAR

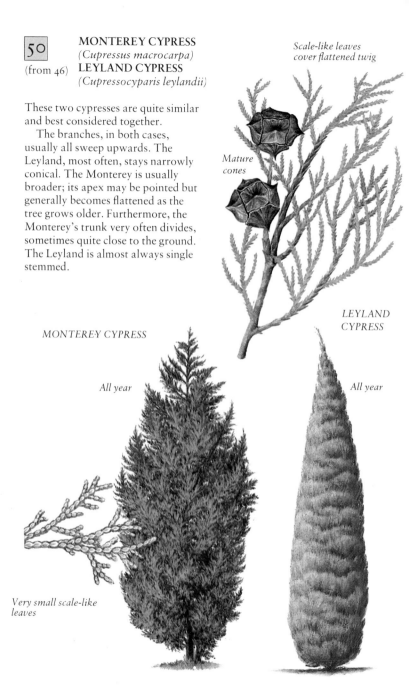

50

(from 46)

MONTEREY CYPRESS
(Cupressus macrocarpa)
LEYLAND CYPRESS
(Cupressocyparis leylandii)

*Scale-like leaves
cover flattened twig*

These two cypresses are quite similar and best considered together.

The branches, in both cases, usually all sweep upwards. The Leyland, most often, stays narrowly conical. The Monterey is usually broader; its apex may be pointed but generally becomes flattened as the tree grows older. Furthermore, the Monterey's trunk very often divides, sometimes quite close to the ground. The Leyland is almost always single stemmed.

Mature cones

LEYLAND CYPRESS

MONTEREY CYPRESS

All year

All year

Very small scale-like leaves

The scale-like leaves of the Monterey cypress, which have a distinctive lemon-like scent if crushed, are so exceedingly small that the foliage is cord-like. The Leyland's are rather larger – very like those of the Lawson cypress (see 48).

The Leyland cypress produces few cones. They almost always grow singly, at the very end of a branch.

The Monterey cypress is often prolific, with many cones in close clusters. The cones of both are brown and leathery, roughly spherical but lumpy. The Monterey's (up to 4cm) tend to be slightly the larger.

Both trees may reach a height of 30m, but are often clipped to form a hedge.

51   Is it evergreen or deciduous?

(from 43)

Deciduous trees are those which lose all their foliage in winter. Evergreens keep their leaves all year. They may almost always be easily distinguished in any season, not only because the leaves of evergreens, except perhaps for young ones that have just come out, are usually an unchanging darker green (though in some species the undersides are paler, almost white), but they are also tougher and stronger.

If you are in any doubt, glance at the evergreens in 53–66 before turning on to 67 if necessary.

Evergreen [52]
Deciduous [67]

52   Do the leaves have pale undersides?

(from 51)

Answer 'Yes' if the undersides of the leaves are covered with fine hairs, giving them a silver-grey, almost white appearance. Otherwise answer 'No'.

Yes [53]   No [54]

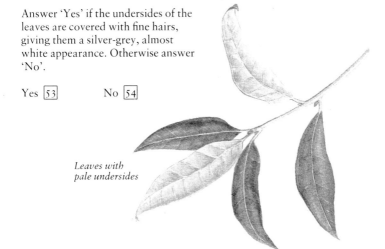

Leaves with pale undersides

HOLM OAK or Holly Oak or Evergreen Oak
(Quercus ilex)

Alternate leaves, sometimes spiny

All year

Acorns

This is by far the commonest of the evergreen oaks to be seen in Britain. You can tell it's an oak if you spot any acorns though, unlike the acorns of the better known oaks, they are more than half hidden by their cups. But the leaves (up to 10cm) are totally different from those of the deciduous species (see 70–71). They are narrow with smooth edges, except on young trees or the lower branches of older trees, when they are often broader and spiny. Their upper surfaces are dark glossy green, but the undersides are felted with hair and very nearly white. The male flowers are drooping yellow catkins.

The holm oak tends to grow with a straight trunk, and a spreading, rounded crown is often formed. It may reach 30m.

| 54 | ## Are the leaves narrow with smooth edges?

(from 52)

Answer 'Yes' if the leaves are at least 2–3 times as long as they are broad, and their margins have no teeth, spines or prickles. Otherwise answer 'No'.

Yes [55]   No [60]

Narrow leaf with smooth edges

55

Is the foliage aromatic?

(from 54)

Answer 'Yes' only if the leaves, when crushed between the fingers, have a pleasant, pungent smell.

Yes 56   No 57

56

BAY LAUREL or Sweet Bay
(Laurus nobilis)

(from 55)

Bay leaves are much in demand for cooking, and also sometimes for wreath-making, so the bay laurel is usually kept trimmed to bush size, but will reach a height of 15–20m if allowed. It is at once distinguished by its aromatic leaves, which are narrow and untoothed. The male and female flowers, which grow on different trees, are yellow and not very noticeable. The female flowers turn into round green berries which have blackened by October.

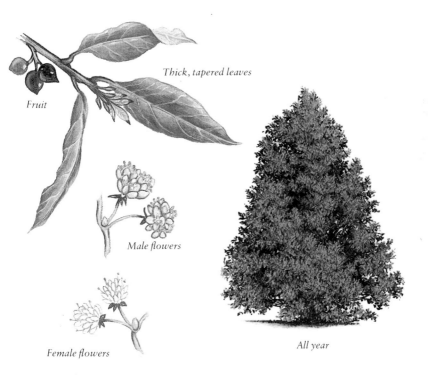

Thick, tapered leaves

Fruit

Male flowers

Female flowers

All year

57 Are the leaves thick and fleshy?

(from 55)

Answer 'Yes' if the leaves, which are only 2–3 times as long as they are broad, have glossy surfaces and are distinctly fleshy; they are thicker than other evergreens'. Otherwise answer 'No'.

Yes 58   No 59

58 EVERGREEN MAGNOLIA or Southern Magnolia
(Magnolia grandiflora)

(from 57)

When in flower, this species is unmistakable, with its exotic, fragrant blooms, which are white and fleshy with a diameter of 15–25cm. Later they develop into conspicuous, hairy fruit. At all times, it may be distinguished by its rather narrow, smooth-edged, leathery leaves, which have rust-red hairs on their undersides and are quite distinct from those of other magnolias, which are deciduous (see 107).

This handsome species is widely planted for decorative purposes and is more often bush-like in appearance. But it may grow into a tree with a height of up to 10m.

Large, fleshy flower

Narrow, leathery leaves with hairy undersides

59 CIDER GUM
(Eucalyptus gunnii)
SNOW GUM
or Tasmanian Snow Gum
(Eucalyptus niphophilia)

(from 57)

Of the many species of gum tree found in their native Australia, these two are most tolerant of Britain's more temperate climate and are therefore most commonly planted.

When the cider gum is young – up to about 4 years – its leaves are

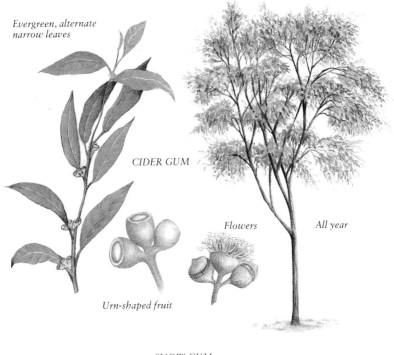

Evergreen, alternate narrow leaves

CIDER GUM

Flowers

All year

Urn-shaped fruit

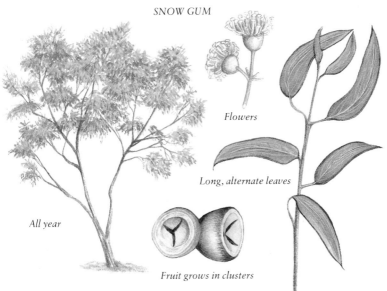

SNOW GUM

Flowers

Long, alternate leaves

All year

Fruit grows in clusters

distinctive in being almost round and stalkless, set in opposite pairs. Otherwise, both species have narrow, smooth-edged leaves. The cider gum's (up to 10cm) grow less long than the snow gum's (up to 14cm) and may have a blueish tinge. The leaf-stalks and leaf-veins of the snow gum tend to be red, whilst those of the other are yellow. Both have similar white flowers turning to hard green fruit.

As with most members of the genus, the bark of both is smooth and usually peels. Its colour varies greatly, but the cider gum's is often grey or orange-red, while the snow gum's is more usually grey-green or blueish with paler streaks.

In Australia the snow gum is often bushy. Here, it usually has a single stem, but tends to be straggly and does not exceed 10m in height. The cider gum normally grows straighter and may approach 30m. Its stem is almost always single, unless it is cut back as a young tree, when several stems will grow to replace it.

How big are the leaves?

(from 52)
This question needs no elaboration.

Not more than 4cm 61
6–10cm 64

Are the leaves sharp and spiny?

(from 60)
Answer 'Yes' if the hard, spiny leaves are roughly triangular, curving quickly to a point, and are set closely in a spiral around their twig. Answer 'No' if the leaves are soft and rather fleshy on short stalks, and grow in opposite pairs.

Yes 62   No 63

62 MONKEY PUZZLE
(*Araucaria araucana*)

(from 61)

This species is always grown decoratively, often in gardens. It is at once recognized by the intricate pattern of its branches, drooping at first but with rising extremities,

Sharp spiny leaves

which form a complex pattern that might indeed puzzle a monkey. As it grows older, all the lower branches may fall off, leaving the trunk bare for almost all its length. The leaves have already been described (see 61). Usually a monkey puzzle carries either male or female cones, not both. The male cones (10–12cm) are egg-shaped and turn from green to reddish-brown. The female cones, which are even larger (up to 15cm), are round and spiny and contain edible seeds. The monkey puzzle reaches 30m.

All year

Mature cone

Thick bark with horizontal rings

Spiny leaves cover branches

MONKEY PUZZLE

| 63 | **BOX** *(Buxus sempervirens)* |

(from 61)

The box is most often seen clipped neatly into hedges or used for topiary, but if left to itself may grow into a sizeable tree, rather rounded in shape, up to 10m in height. Its timber is used for carving.

It is easily distinguished by its small evergreen leaves (12–30mm in length), which are oval, short-stalked and usually have notched tips. Its small yellow flowers grow in little groups at the bases of the leaves. Later they develop into three-horned seed capsules. The bark of younger trees is light brown. This turns grey with age, and may become cracked into irregular square plates.

Oval evergreen leaves

Fruit

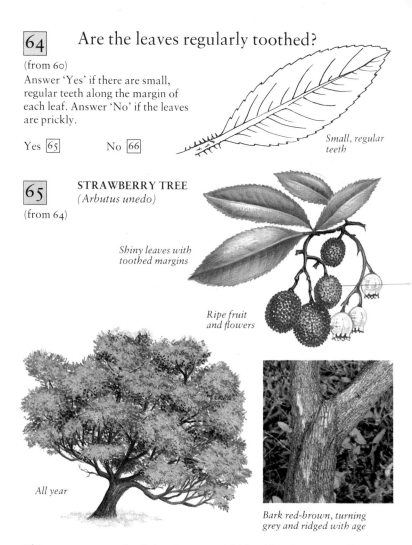

64 Are the leaves regularly toothed?

(from 60)

Answer 'Yes' if there are small,
regular teeth along the margin of
each leaf. Answer 'No' if the leaves
are prickly.

Yes [65]   No [66]

Small, regular teeth

65 STRAWBERRY TREE
(Arbutus unedo)

(from 64)

Shiny leaves with toothed margins

Ripe fruit and flowers

All year

Bark red-brown, turning grey and ridged with age

This uncommon species derives its
name from its unmistakable fruit,
which somewhat resembles a wild
strawberry. It takes a year to ripen
from green to scarlet and is edible
but not tasty. The flowers are also
very distinctive. They come out in
the late autumn, when the previous
year's fruit is just ripening. White or
pinkish-white, they are small (6mm)
and bell-shaped, hanging in clusters
of up to 20. The toothed leaves are
narrow and pointed.

The strawberry tree is often bush-
like in appearance, but may reach
12m. It is commonest in south-west
Ireland, where it grows wild. Also
planted in gardens.

HOLLY
(Ilex aquifolium)

(from 64)

The holly quite often grows as a
bush, or may be trimmed into a
hedge, but it can grow into a well-
shaped, conical tree, well over 10m in
height.

It is very easy to recognize with its
well-known prickly leaves – though
some may be almost or wholly
spineless – and, in autumn and
winter, its much-prized red berries,
though these grow only on female
trees. The small white flowers of
both sexes are inconspicuous.

Many varieties of holly have been
cultivated, which may have
varicoloured leaves (usually green
and yellow, sometimes without
prickles) or yellow berries, but these
are beyond the scope of this book.

*Prickly,
shiny leaves*

All year

*Berries, only on
female trees*

*Bark, green when young;
greys with maturity*

Are the leaves simple or compound?

(from 51)

Simple leaves are much the more usual. Each leaf is single: that is to say, it is not made up of several smaller leaves or leaflets.

Relatively few species have compound leaves. Each of these has at least three leaflets – often many more. Either these leaflets are arranged, usually in pairs, along each side of their mid-rib (illustration A), or they spread out from the end of their leaf-stalk to form the shape of a fan (illustration B). Choose your answer accordingly.

Simple [68]
Compound [153]

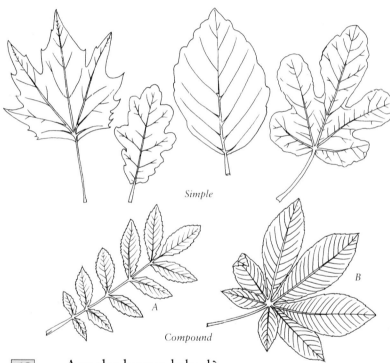

Simple

Compound

A

B

68 Are the leaves lobed?

(from 67)

Lobes, which may be rounded or pointed, are conspicuous projections (not mere teeth) in the margins of leaves. They are of two distinct kinds.

If leaves are *pinnately* lobed, like the oak's, the lobes run irregularly along the margins. Such leaves always have a single central vein, from which parallel side-veins extend to the tip of each lobe.

If they are *palmately* lobed, like the maple's, the lobes are more regular and radiate. They are pointed and may be toothed. In most cases, they have veins running from the tip of each lobe to a point at or near the base of the leaf, where they unite.

You should have no difficulty in telling from the drawings whether your leaf is lobed; and, if so, whether pinnately or palmately. Choose your answer accordingly.

Yes – pinnately [69]

    – palmately [72]

No [93]

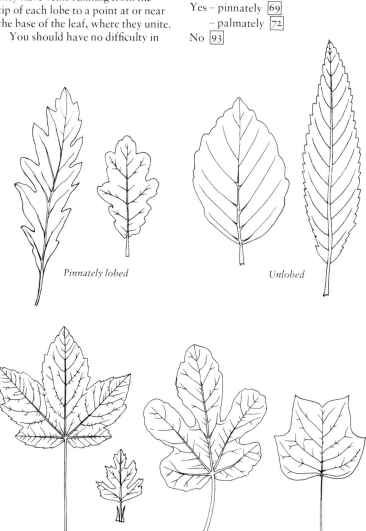

Pinnately lobed

Unlobed

Palmately lobed

(from 68)

Answer 'Yes' if the lobes are rounded and rather shallow; they make quite a regular pattern along the margin of each leaf. Answer 'No' if they tend to be more irregular and cut deeply into the leaf margins.

Yes 70   No 71

Rounded lobes   *Deeply cut lobes*

70

ENGLISH OAK or Pendunculate Oak or Common Oak
(Quercus robur)

(from 69) **SESSILE OAK or Durmast Oak**
(Quercus petraea)

ENGLISH OAK

These are the only oaks native to Britain and are generally more common than the many introduced species. It is quite easy to confuse them.

Stalked acorns

The leaves are similar in shape. The main difference is that those of the sessile oak have very distinct stalks (1–2cm), whilst the other's are stalkless or nearly so. It's the other way round with the acorns – and with the inconspicuous female flowers from which they develop. These are completely stalkless in the sessile oak, but the English oak's have long stalks (4–8cm). In springtime both species have similar male flowers, hanging in bunches of yellow catkins.

Lobed, stalkless leaves

The shape of many trees can vary greatly, and this is very much the case with these two species. A lone tree usually has a short, stout base, spreading quickly into many sizeable branches to form an extensive, rounded crown, which may reach quite close to the ground. But close-grown oaks may have well over 20m of perfectly straight trunk which is completely or nearly branchless. The bark of both species is similar, with regular, deeply-ridged, vertical fissures, except in young trees when these are absent or much less noticeable.

Summer

Winter

ENGLISH OAK

Summer

SESSILE OAK

Stalked leaves

Acorns without stalks

TURKEY OAK
(Quercus cerris)

Of the half-dozen oaks occurring in Britain whose leaves have deeply-cut or pointed lobes, this is the only species well enough known to justify inclusion.

It is at once recognized by its unusually narrow leaves (up to 12cm) with their 4–9 pairs of deep, jagged lobes. They are glossy green above and downy grey below. The male flowers are drooping yellow catkins. The inconspicuous female flowers develop into large acorns (up to 25mm), which are half hidden by their unusual shaggy cups.

Turkey oak is not favoured for use as timber but is quite widely planted ornamentally. It usually develops a clean, straight trunk with deep vertical fissures and has reached 40m.

Alternate deeply cut lobed leaves

Catkins

Female flower

Autumn leaves

Acorns in shaggy cups

Summer

Rough, fissured bark

72   Are the leaves opposite or alternate?

(from 68)

The maples, which include the sycamore, are distinguished by having their leaves in opposite pairs. All other species covered in this section have leaves that grow alternately. Choose your answer accordingly.

Opposite 73   Alternate 80

Alternate

Opposite

73   How big are the leaves?

(from 72)

Of the five best-known maples included, two have relatively small leaves (5–7cm), whilst those of the three others are appreciably larger. Leaves always vary in size, so select an average one to help you make your choice.

5–7cm 74   Well over 7cm 77

74   Are the lobes long and pointed?

(from 73)

Turn to 75 if the lobes are noticeably long and pointed, with many sharp teeth. Choose 76 if they are more rounded with a few blunt indentations. The illustrations should leave you in no doubt.

Yes 75   No 76

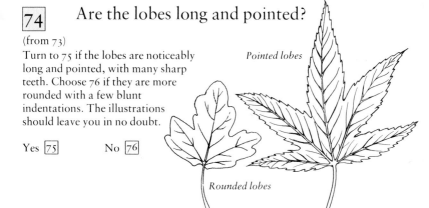

Pointed lobes

Rounded lobes

JAPANESE MAPLE
(Acer palmatum)

75

(from 74)

The delicate, sharply-pointed leaves of this species, which have 5–7 lobes, are very distinctive and should make recognition easy. They turn reddish purple in autumn.

The Japanese maple is often more shrub-like than the other maples, with a short, smooth-barked trunk usually dividing into upswept branches. It reaches a height of 15m. Many cultivars of this species have been developed.

Leaves with pointed lobes

Summer

Flowers

Winged fruits

FIELD MAPLE
(Acer campestre)

76

(from 74)

The only other well-known maple with such small leaves, this species is clearly distinct from the Japanese maple (see 75) because the 3–5 lobes of the leaves do not have sharp tips. They turn yellowish-orange in autumn. The winged seeds common to all maples are distinctive: each pair grows almost at right angles to its stalk, forming a nearly straight line. At first they are green, perhaps with a pink tinge; later they turn brown.

The field maple is most often seen in hedgerows in southern England, where it is generally closely clipped, but many trees are allowed to grow on, and may reach 25m. The bark is greyish-brown with shallow cracks and fissures.

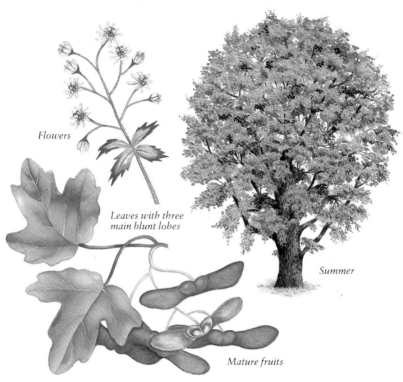

Flowers

Leaves with three main blunt lobes

Summer

Mature fruits

77 Are the leaves very deeply divided?

(from 73)

Answer 'Yes' if the 3–7 lobes, which are narrow and sharply-toothed, are so deeply divided that they form well over half the total length of each leaf. Otherwise answer 'No'.

Yes 78
No 79

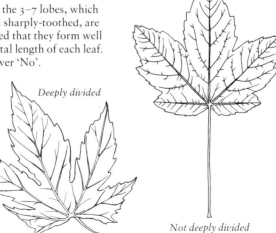

Deeply divided

Not deeply divided

78 SILVER MAPLE
(*Acer saccharinum*)
(from 77)

Summer

*Toothed leaves with
five deeply divided lobes*

Flower

Fruit

The silver maple is best recognized by its deeply-lobed leaves, which in spring and summer are glossy green above and silver-grey below. In autumn, they turn to lovely shades of yellow, sometimes red. Small reddish flowers come out in March before the leaves. They may develop into the winged seeds typical of the maples.

The trunk has smooth grey bark, which often becomes flaky. The tree may reach 30m. In its native North America it is used for commercial sugar production; even in Britain, small quantities of syrup may be obtained.

79 SYCAMORE
(*Acer pseudoplatanus*)
(from 77) **NORWAY MAPLE**
(*Acer platanoides*)

These two species have similar leaves, usually with five well-defined, pointed lobes, but those of the sycamore, which is much the more common, have smaller, blunter teeth. The leaves vary greatly in size, but the sycamore's tend to be larger (up to 18cm) than the other's (up to 12cm). In both cases they are often broader than they are long.

The flowers are distinctive, though always small and yellow. The

Winter

Leaves and flowers

Fruit in pairs forming right angle

SYCAMORE

Pointed lobes

NORWAY MAPLE

Winter

Flowers and mature fruit in pairs forming straight line

Norway maple's open before the leaves, in early April, growing from erect stalks in groups of 20–30. The sycamore's come out later, with the leaves, and hang downwards in clusters of up to 50 or even more. Both species have the winged seeds, growing in pairs, that are typical of maples. The sycamore's pairs tend to form a right angle, whilst those of the Norway maple are in more of a straight line.

The Norway maple's bark develops a network of fine ridges, mostly vertical. The sycamore's is quite unfissured, and has a very noticeable tendency to flake off, except in younger trees. Both species reach timber size quite quickly, but the Norway maple tends to be more slender and grows less tall (27m) than the sycamore (35m). They are much prized for veneers if the tree has grown cleanly.

80 Are the leaves small?

(from 72)

Choose 81 if most fully-grown leaves are no more than 4–5cm in length. Turn to 84 if, except in some isolated cases, they are appreciably longer.

Yes 81   No 84

81 Are its flowers white or red?

(from 80)

Should no blooms be visible, it is almost certain to have been white-flowered if berries are present. If in doubt, consult both entries.

White 82   Red 83

82 COMMON HAWTHORN or May or Quickthorn
(*Crataegus monogyna*)

(from 81) **MIDLAND HAWTHORN**
(*Crataegus laevigata*)

These two closely related species are very similar and care must be taken in distinguishing between them.

The leaves of the common hawthorn have more deeply divided lobes than the Midland's, which tend to be more rounded and sometimes larger. In both species, the masses of small white flowers are very conspicuous in May and June. Those of the common hawthorn are smaller (8–15mm) than the Midland's

(15–25mm). When these become berries – green at first, then scarlet – the common hawthorn's are smaller and rounder. If crushed between the fingers, they are found to contain one seed, while the Midland's berry has two.

Both species have very sharp thorns and both may reach 10m. The common hawthorn is widely used for hedging.

Flower

Summer

Winter

COMMON HAWTHORN

Lobed, toothed leaves and ripe berries

Shiny lobed leaves

Flowers

MIDLAND HAWTHORN

Ripe berries

Summer

83   RED HAWTHORN
(Crataegus laevigata varieties)

(from 81)

A number of red-flowered varieties of the Midland hawthorn have been cultivated, too numerous to describe in detail. Apart from the instantly noticeable colour of their blooms, they closely resemble the Midland but very seldom form berries.

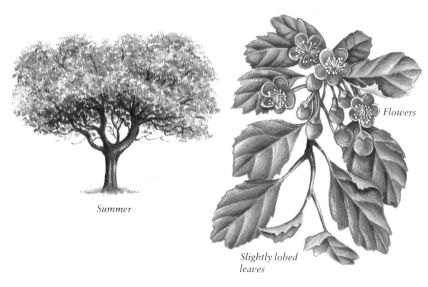

Summer

Flowers

Slightly lobed leaves

84   Do the leaves have hairs?

(from 80)

Answer 'Yes' if the leaves are hairy or downy, though perhaps only on their undersides. Late in the season the down may become so sparse that it is visible to the naked eye only on the veins. Answer 'No' if both sides of the leaves are absolutely hairless, except perhaps when they are very young.

Yes 85   No 88

85   Are the leaves very large?

(from 84)

Turn to 86 if the leaves are extremely large (up to 30cm) and with rounded lobes. Choose 87 if they are maple-like and no more than 10cm long.

Yes 86   No 87

FIG
(Ficus carica)

(from 85)

The fig barely qualifies as a tree in Britain, where it is usually grown against a south-facing wall, developing several stems and usually not exceeding 3–4m in height. But some specimens may reach 8m, with a single smooth, grey trunk, soon dividing into many spreading branches. Apart from its well-known fruit, it is recognized by its very large, deeply-divided leaves, which are hairy and have 3–5 rounded lobes with small teeth. They often grow in profusion.

The species is unusual in having no visible flowers. When the future fruit first appears, it already resembles a small green fig. It takes two summers to swell and grow, becoming gradually softer and turning purple-black.

Mature fruit

Leathery, lobed hairy leaves

Summer

Pale grey bark with darker streaks

87

(from 85)

WHITE POPLAR or Abele
(Populus alba)

Hairy leaves with white undersides

Mature male catkins

Mature female catkins

Winter

This is alone among the poplars in having palmate leaves (up to 9cm) with 3–5 very distinct lobes, except on the lower branches, where the lobes may be much less marked. In both cases, the leaves are distinguished by being thickly covered, when young, with soft white down. This is quickly lost on their upper surfaces, which become smooth and green. Their undersides stay white and hairy, though less noticeably.

Male and female catkins grow on separate trees. They appear before the leaves, usually in March. The former turn scarlet; the latter are green and more elongated, becoming fluffy with white seeds. White poplars may reach 25m.

Does it have maple-like leaves?

(from 84)

Answer 'Yes' if it has leaves with
five pointed, toothed lobes
(occasionally with three or seven
lobes) resembling those of a
maple. Veins run from the point of
each lobe to unite at the base of the
leaf. Answer 'No' if it has four
untoothed lobes (occasionally six). A
central vein bisects the leaf, with
parallel side-veins joining it.

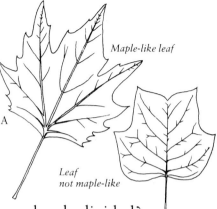

Maple-like leaf

*Leaf
not maple-like*

Yes 89   No 92

89   Are the leaves very deeply divided?

(from 88)

Answer 'Yes' if most of the lobes are
at least twice as long as they are
broad. Otherwise answer 'No'. The
illustrations should make it easy for
you to decide.

Yes 90   No 91

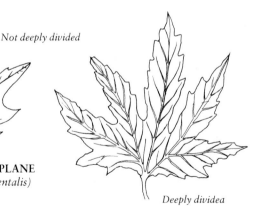

Not deeply divided

Deeply divided

90   ORIENTAL PLANE
(Platanus orientalis)

(from 89)

The oriental plane is much less
widely planted than the well-known
London plane (see 91), of which it is
probably an ancestor. It is
distinguished from it by its leaves,
which are much more deeply divided
and may have 7 lobes (more usually

5); by its fruit, which grows in
clusters of 3–6 and, though also
spherical, is more spiny; and by its
trunk, which usually divides sooner
than the London plane's and
therefore tends to be shorter. Does
not exceed 30m.

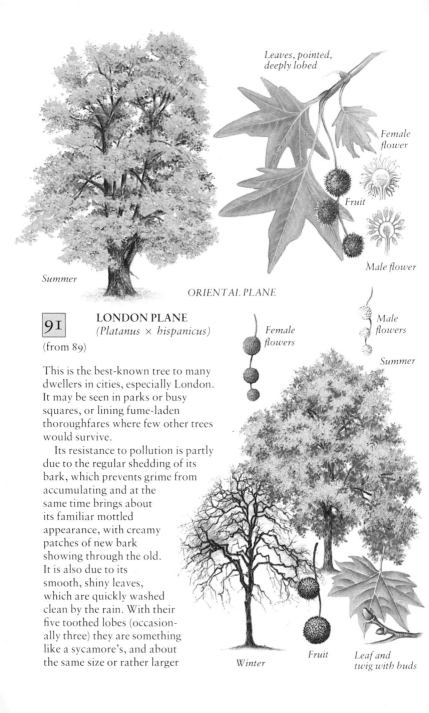

Leaves, pointed, deeply lobed

Female flower

Fruit

Male flower

ORIENTAL PLANE

9 1 **LONDON PLANE**
(Platanus × hispanicus)

(from 89)

This is the best-known tree to many dwellers in cities, especially London. It may be seen in parks or busy squares, or lining fume-laden thoroughfares where few other trees would survive.

Its resistance to pollution is partly due to the regular shedding of its bark, which prevents grime from accumulating and at the same time brings about its familiar mottled appearance, with creamy patches of new bark showing through the old. It is also due to its smooth, shiny leaves, which are quickly washed clean by the rain. With their five toothed lobes (occasion- ally three) they are something like a sycamore's, and about the same size or rather larger

Female flowers

Male flowers

Summer

Winter

Fruit

Leaf and twig with buds

(up to 20cm). But they differ by growing alternately instead of in opposing pairs.

Male and female flowers, spherical in both cases, grow singly or in clusters of 2–4. The females are reddish-brown, each on a single stalk at the very end of a twig. The males are green and smaller, growing nearby on the same tree. The brown 'bobbles' of the ripe fruit stay on the tree all winter.

London planes usually have a long, straight trunk, unbranched, or nearly so, for much of its length, and may reach 45m.

92 **TULIP TREE**
(*Liriodendron tulipifera*)
(from 88)

This very handsome tree, which may reach 35m, is among the easiest to recognize. Apart from its showy flowers, which are like greenish-yellow tulips, it is alone in having leaves (up to 15cm) that come to four distinct points – or very occasionally six. They have long stalks (5–10cm) and are hairless and untoothed.

The tree in most cases has a long single trunk, but sometimes this will divide. Its branches tend not to spread, so that it may have an almost poplar-like outline. The leaves turn yellow in autumn and stay on the tree very late in the year, even till after Christmas.

Summer

Pointed leaves

Tulip-like flowers

Young fruit

N.B.

Are the leaves pointed at each end?

(from 68)

Answer 'Yes' only if each leaf comes to a point at each end, usually more pronounced at the apex than at the base. Otherwise go on to 121. Note that the very common beech has rather variable leaves. They always have a very pointed tip; but their base, when it isn't rounded, could hardly be thought pointed either – see 152.

Yes 94   No 121

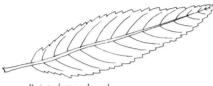

Pointed at each end

Not pointed at each end

Are its leaves at least four times longer than broad?

(from 93)

If necessary, take the measurements of a typical leaf to decide on the right answer.

Yes 95   No 100

Is it 'weeping'?

(from 94)

Trees are said to be 'weeping' if their branches for the most part droop downwards, sometimes vertically at their extremities, so that they touch the ground or come close to doing so.

Yes 96   No 97

Weeping branches

CHINESE WEEPING WILLOW
(Salix babylonica)

(from 95) **GOLDEN WEEPING WILLOW**
(Salix × chrysocoma)

Many different weeping willows are grown in the British Isles, but these two are much the commonest and are the only ones included.

The golden weeping willow, a hybrid, is now the more often seen. It is easily distinguished from all others by its golden-yellow boughs and twigs, specially noticeable when the tree is bare in winter. Its hairy leaves seldom exceed 10cm.

Apart from its brown bark, the Chinese weeping willow may be distinguished from the golden hybrid by its hairless leaves, which grow much longer (16cm) and are less noticeably toothed.

Both trees have yellow catkins and reach a height of some 20m.

Summer

Catkin

Long slender, finely toothed leaves, pale undersides

CHINESE WEEPING WILLOW

GOLDEN WEEPING WILLOW

Summer

Catkins

Long toothed leaves

(from 95)
Answer 'Yes' if the leaves have silky hairs on both surfaces, especially the undersides. Answer 'No' if they are completely hairless, except when very young.

Yes 98   No 99

98   WHITE WILLOW
(Salix alba)

(from 97)

Summer

Female catkin with fluffy seeds

Finely toothed pointed leaves, hairy undersides

White willows are best distinguished by their leaves (up to 8cm), which are blue-green above and silver-grey below. They are finely toothed. Male and female catkins (both up to 5cm) always grow on separate trees; the former are yellow, the latter green, later becoming fluffy with white seed. They first appear in April or May.

This species may reach a considerable height for a willow – up to 25m – but is often pollarded. The bark grows in a network of ridges.

Many varieties of the white willow have been cultivated, but these are beyond the scope of this book.

This species is distinguished by its very brittle twigs, which break off easily with a 'crack'. The leaves (up to 12cm long) are hairless, except when very young. They are shiny green above, grey-green below, and have rather fine teeth.

Male and female catkins are always found on separate trees; the former are yellow (2–5cm), whilst the latter may reach 10cm and are greenish, later becoming fluffy with white seed. They first appear in April.

Crack willows often grow by streams. They may grow as high as 24m, but are often pollarded. As they grow older, their bark becomes quite deeply ridged.

Female catkins

Summer

Shiny brittle leaves

100
(from 94)

Are the leaves at least twice as long as broad?

Again, take the measurements of a typical leaf, if necessary, to decide on the right answer.

Yes 101   No 116

101
(from 100)

Do the leaves have hairy undersides?

Answer 'Yes' if the undersides of the leaves are covered with hairs or down. Answer 'No' if they are hairless, except perhaps on the veins.

Yes 102   No 108

102
(from 101)

Do the leaves have toothed margins?

Choose 103 if there are teeth, however fine, along the margin of each leaf. Otherwise turn to 107.

Yes 103   No 107

Toothed margin   *Untoothed margin*

103
(from 102)

Is it thorny?

Answer 'Yes' if occasional very sharp, woody thorns, sometimes several centimetres long, protrude at intervals from its twigs and branches.

Otherwise answer 'No'.

Yes 104   No 105

104
(from 103)

BLACKTHORN or Sloe
(Prunus spinosa)

The blackthorn generally grows as a bush or is clipped into a hedge, but it can become a small tree up to 6m in height.

It is most noticeable and easy to recognize in March or April, when it is covered with small white flowers up to 15mm in diameter, before the appearance of the leaves. Later the flowers develop into small green berries (sloes), which remain very bitter as they ripen to blue-black. The leaves are small (up to 4cm) with hairy undersides. They vary in shape and their bases, in particular, may not be very noticeably pointed.

The blackthorn usually grows in a tangle of thorny branches which are difficult to penetrate.

Summer

Ripe sloes

Toothed leaves

Flowers

105   Does it have very big leaves?

(from 103)

Answer 'Yes' if the leaves, which have deep teeth and are rather glossy, are seldom less than 10cm in length and in most cases much longer – up to 25cm. Answer 'No' in all other cases.

Yes 111   No 106

106   MEDLAR
(Mespilus germanica)

(from 105)

The medlar's leaves (up to 15cm) are about three times as long as they are broad. They are finely toothed, but the teeth do not run the full length of each margin. Their underside is noticeably downy. They may turn russet in autumn.

The flower (3–4cm) is very distinctive, appearing in early summer. It is stalkless and grows singly at the very end of its twig, with five pure white petals – and five long

Summer

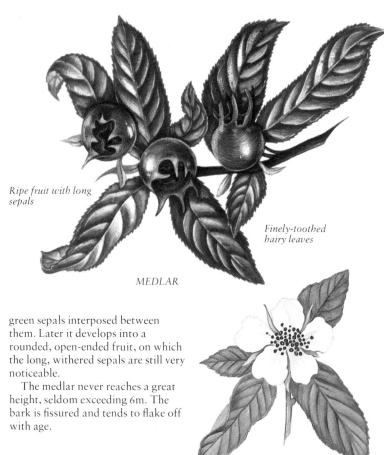

Ripe fruit with long sepals

Finely-toothed hairy leaves

MEDLAR

green sepals interposed between them. Later it develops into a rounded, open-ended fruit, on which the long, withered sepals are still very noticeable.

The medlar never reaches a great height, seldom exceeding 6m. The bark is fissured and tends to flake off with age.

Flower

107	**MAGNOLIA**

(Magnolia × soulangeana)

(from 102)

This hybrid is the best known of the deciduous magnolias. All members of the family have large exotic blooms, usually pinkish-white, but the others, except the evergreen magnolia (see 57), are too seldom seen for inclusion in this book.

The fragrant blooms, with 6–9 petals, are the magnolia's most distinctive feature. These come out in April, before the leaves, and may

reach 25cm in diameter. They develop into reddish-brown cone-like fruit. The untoothed leaves are quite deeply veined and up to 15cm in length. They have noticeably downy undersides.

This magnolia is most often bush-like in appearance, or may be trained against a wall, but in a favourable position it will grow into a tree and sometimes reaches 10m.

Summer

Downy pointed leaves

MAGNOLIA

Flower

Downy bud

108
(from 101)

Are the leaves opposite or alternate?

The leaves of most trees grow singly, on alternate sides of their twigs, but in some cases they are in opposing pairs along it. Choose your answer accordingly.

Opposite 109
Alternate 110

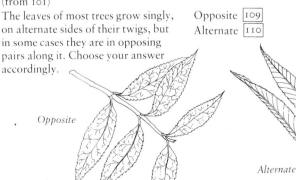

Opposite

Alternate

109

(from 108)

SPINDLE TREE
(*Euonymus europaeus*)

This is the only species likely to be seen with narrow, toothed leaves that grow in opposite pairs.

It only just qualifies as a tree because it rarely exceeds 6m and often, but not always, has several

Flowers

Ripe fruits

Autumn leaves, pointed, finely-toothed

N.E.

Autumn

independent trunks or stems rising from near the ground, which give it a shrubby appearance. The leaves (up to 10cm) are very finely toothed and hairless. The small 4-petalled flowers are pale yellow and grow in groups of 3–8. Later they ripen into conspicuous 4-lobed fruits, each lobe containing a seed. They turn from green to pink.

110

(from 108)

Does it have very big leaves?

Answer 'Yes' if the leaves, which have deep teeth and are rather glossy, are seldom less than 10cm in length and in most cases much longer – up to 25cm. Answer 'No' in all other cases.

Yes [111]   No [112]

III

(from 105 and 110)

SPANISH CHESTNUT or Sweet Chestnut
(Castanea sativa)

Winter

Bark spirals up trunk

Spiny fruit open in autumn to release nuts

Pointed, toothed leaves with parallel veins; turn orangey-brown in autumn

Nut

The leaves of this handsome species make it easy to recognize: they are narrow, pointed, very long and sharply toothed. When they first come out, their undersides are downy, but soon they become hairless. The male flowers are long yellow catkins (up to 15cm), which always appear after the leaves. The well-known fruits grow in groups of two or three and have very prickly

spines. Each fruit is up to 4cm in diameter and usually contains 2–3 edible brown nuts.

The Spanish chestnut grows to be a large forest tree up to 30m high. It has characteristic bark – deeply ridged, often spirally. Its leaves, flowers, fruit and bark are very different from the horse chestnut (see 156), which bears the rounder inedible nuts used as 'conkers'.

Do the branches tend to be horizontal?

Answer 'Yes' if most of the branches grow more or less horizontally for the greater part of their length. Answer 'No' if they are mostly at a pronounced angle to the stem.

Yes | 113 | No | 114 |

Horizontal branches

SNOWBELL TREE
(Styrax japonica)

When in bloom, this decorative tree is at once known by its flowers (25mm) with their pointed white petals and yellow stamens; or later by its fruits (15mm) which are egg-shaped and hang in small groups in long stalks, turning from green to brown.

The snowbell tree may also be recognized by its narrow, pointed leaves (up to 8cm), which are very finely toothed and, in all seasons, by its branches, which grow so stiffly horizontal that the tree is often less high than it is wide. It seldom exceeds 8m.

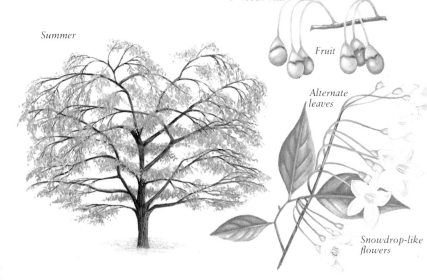

Summer

Fruit

Alternate leaves

Snowdrop-like flowers

Are the leaves very narrow?

(from 112)

Turn to 115 if the leaves are much more than twice as long as they are broad – perhaps almost four times. Otherwise it is most likely to be a cherry and you should go on to 140.

Yes | 115 | No | 144 |

| 115 |

ALMOND
(Prunus dulcis)

(from 114)

This decorative species is easy to recognize in early spring, when its delicate pink flowers (3–5cm) are among the first to appear. They come out before the leaves in March or April, usually singly or in pairs. Later, they form oval green fruits with a velvety texture (up to 4cm), which may ripen even in Britain to produce the much-prized nuts.

The almond's leaves (7–12cm) are very narrow and finely toothed. Like the cherry's, its bark is often ringed with horizontal bands of breathing pores. It grows to 9m and its timber is used for joinery and veneers.

Summer

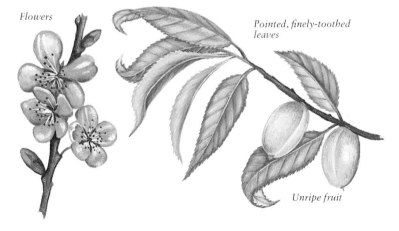

Flowers

Pointed, finely-toothed leaves

Unripe fruit

116   Do the leaves have downy undersides?

(from 100)
Answer 'Yes' if the underside of each
leaf, and sometimes the upper
surface as well, is so covered in fine
hair or down that it looks quite
white, especially early in the season.   Yes 117   No 118

117   WHITEBEAM
         (Sorbus aria)

(from 116)

The whitebeam has conspicuous
creamy-white flowers, about 15mm
in diameter. They grow in clusters
from woolly stalks and later develop
into crimson berries (up to 15mm),
which may be either rounded or oval.
    The leaves are rather bluntly
pointed, with irregularly toothed
margins. When they first come out,

Summer

Flowers

Ripe berries

*Pointed, toothed
leaves, downy undersides*

both surfaces are densely covered with downy white hair, so that their texture is rather like felt. Later, this is lost on the upper surface, but the underside stays white till the leaves turn brown or yellow in autumn.

The whitebeam may grow to 25m and usually has upswept branches and a domed crown. The bark of young trees is smooth and quite dark grey. Ridges and scales develop with age.

118 Do its leaves have sharp, regular teeth?

(from 116)

Answer 'Yes' if the teeth, though small, are sharp and regular. Answer 'No' if they are blunt or barely visible, perhaps not extending the full length of the leaf.

Yes 119   No 120

119

(from 118)

CRAB APPLE
(*Malus sylvestris*)
COMMON PEAR or Wild Pear
(*Pyrus communis*)

The many trees that are normally grown only in orchards for their fruit are not included in this book. Among them are many commercial varieties of apple and pear, whose fruit is so well known. These have often been developed from the two above

COMMON PEAR
Summer

CRAB APPLE
Summer

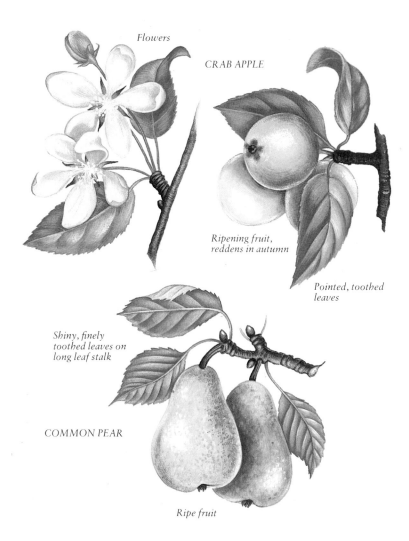

Flowers

CRAB APPLE

Ripening fruit,
reddens in autumn

Pointed, toothed
leaves

Shiny, finely
toothed leaves on
long leaf stalk

COMMON PEAR

Ripe fruit

species, which both grow wild and are to be found in woods and hedgerows, seldom in gardens.

In spring, these two wild species are easily distinguished because the flowers of the common pear are pure white, whilst the crab apple's have pink undersides. In both cases they develop into fruit that is equally distinctive – very like that of the cultivated varieties, though almost always smaller.

Both species have similar leaves, but the crab apple's are less glossy and a lighter green, whilst the pear's have smaller teeth. The latter tree may reach a greater height (up to 15m) than the former (9m).

GREAT SALLOW or Goat Willow or Pussy Willow
(Salix caprea)

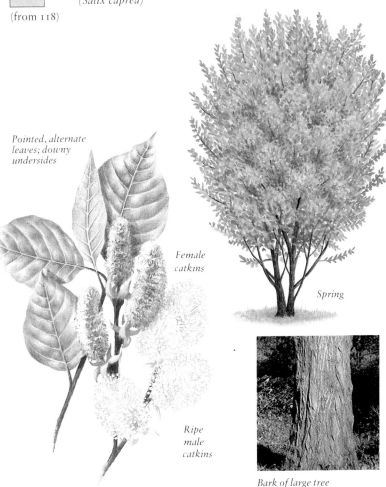

Pointed, alternate leaves; downy undersides

Female catkins

Spring

Ripe male catkins

Bark of large tree

This species is the only well-known member of the willow family with leaves less than twice as long as they are broad. It presents some difficulty beause it hybridizes freely with other willows and there are many intermediate forms.

The great sallow is most noticeable in the very early spring, usually March, when its male catkins – the kind known as 'pussy willows' – come out long before its leaves, and stand out in the bare countryside. The leaves (5–10cm) may have a few blunt teeth and their undersides are hairy. Often bush-like in appearance but may grow to the size of a true tree, sometimes reaching 15m.

What shape is the leaf?

(from 93)

Carefully consider if the leaf has one of the three special features set out below.

Turn to 122 if the leaf, whatever its general shape, is just about as *broad as it is long.*

AS BROAD AS LONG

HEART-SHAPED

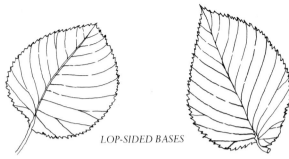

LOP-SIDED BASES

Turn to 129 if it is very noticeably *heart-shaped*, with an indentation at the base, rounded margins and a pointed apex.

Choose 138 if it has a markedly *lop-sided base*: each side joins the leaf stalk at a slightly different point, or one side is much more rounded than the other.

Go on to 142 if the leaf has none of these features.

About as broad as long 122
Heart-shaped 129
Lop-sided base 138
None of the above 142

122   Does each leaf come to a point?

(from 121)

Answer 'Yes' if each leaf comes to a point, however small. Answer 'No' if its tip is rounded – or if there is an indentation where a point might be expected.

Yes 123   No 128

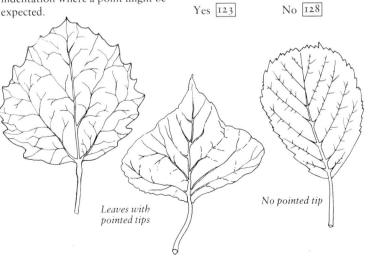

Leaves with pointed tips

No pointed tip

(from 122)

Answer 'Yes' if the margins of each leaf have prominent, straight-sided teeth, which vary widely in size. Answer 'No' if the margins are wavy, or if their teeth (if any) are rounded or very small.

Yes [124]   No [125]

Irregular teeth

Rounded teeth

124   HAZEL
(Corylus avellana)

(from 123)

The hazel is best known for its edible nuts, called cobs, which grow in groups of 1–4 and ripen to a dark brown colour. They develop from very small, seldom-noticed female flowers. The conspicuous male flowers, which grow on the same tree, are drooping yellow catkins up to 5cm long. Each year these are welcomed, as early as February, as one of the first signs of spring. The leaves (up to 10cm) are hairy, especially on their upper surfaces. They are irregularly toothed and very variable in shape, but always have a small but noticeable tip.

Hazels are often used for hedging, or are coppiced. Even if left to themselves, they tend to be shrub-like with several stems, but just manage to qualify as trees, since they sometimes grow with a single stem and may reach 10m.

Hairy, toothed leaves

Autumn leaf

Nuts, partly covered by bracts

Summer

Answer 'Yes' if the tree's branches grow almost vertically upwards, giving it an unmistakably long and narrow outline. Otherwise answer 'No'.

Yes [126]   No [127]

This well-known tree, so often planted along the roads of France, but also widely grown in Britain, is at once recognized by its long, narrow outline, with all its branches sweeping almost vertically upward.

Its hairless leaves are roughly triangular and at least as broad as they are long. They have regular small teeth, except perhaps along their bases.

The Lombardy poplar grows quickly and reaches a height of 30m.

Long narrow outline

Alternate, pointed leaves

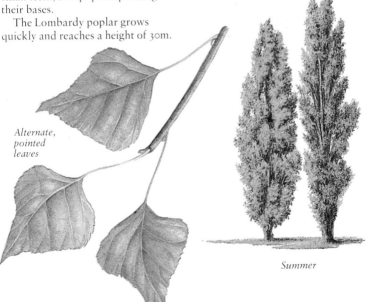

Summer

ASPEN
(Populus tremula)
GREY POPLAR
(Populus canescens)

These two closely related species may be confused because their leaves vary in shape and change texture with the season.

The aspen's most noticeable feature is that its leaves have flat stalks, and this causes them to tremble in the slightest breath of wind. The grey poplar's leaf-stalks are only slightly flattened, if at all. Its leaves may be slightly longer than they are broad, while the aspen's are more rounded – except for those growing from young shoots, which may be heart-shaped or triangular. In both cases, the leaf margins have a few rounded teeth or are wavy.

When the leaves of the aspen first come out, they are copper-coloured and downy, but soon become green and hairless, and then turn yellow in autumn. Those of the grey poplar begin by being so covered in fine hairs that they are white. Unlike the aspen's, only their upper surface becomes hairless. The down stays on the under surface; it becomes less noticeable, but the leaves are still grey underneath.

Both species are often found on

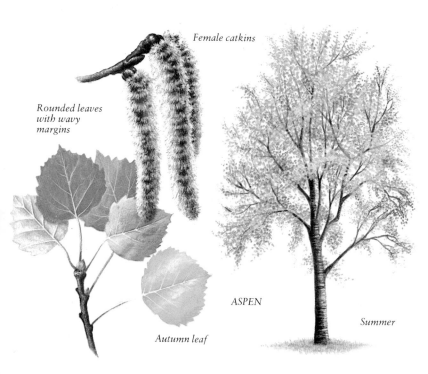

Female catkins

Rounded leaves with wavy margins

Autumn leaf

ASPEN

Summer

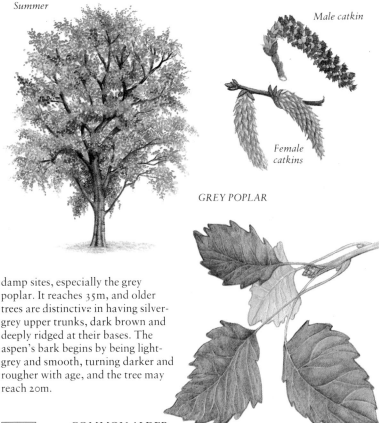

Summer

Male catkin

Female catkins

GREY POPLAR

damp sites, especially the grey poplar. It reaches 35m, and older trees are distinctive in having silver-grey upper trunks, dark brown and deeply ridged at their bases. The aspen's bark begins by being light-grey and smooth, turning darker and rougher with age, and the tree may reach 20m.

128

COMMON ALDER
(Alnus glutinosa)

(from 122)

Leaves from upper branches have more pointed leaves

The almost round leaves of the common alder are distinctive in that they never come to even the slightest point. Indeed, they often have a slight indentation where the point might be expected. The leaf margins are toothed, except sometimes at their bases.

The alder's dangling male catkins (up to 5cm) are purplish-brown. They appear in March before the leaves. The females are at first much less noticeable; they develop into oval green fruits (up to 15mm), which later turn black and woody, looking like small cones. They stay on the tree all winter.

Usually found on damp sites, the alder regenerates freely and may grow rapidly, but does not exceed 25m. (Illustrated on next page.)

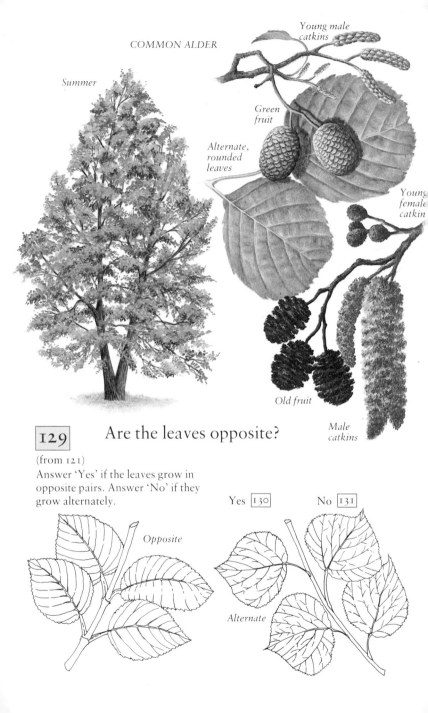

COMMON ALDER

Summer

Young male catkins

Green fruit

Alternate, rounded leaves

Young female catkin

Old fruit

Male catkins

129

Are the leaves opposite?

(from 121)

Answer 'Yes' if the leaves grow in opposite pairs. Answer 'No' if they grow alternately.

Yes 130

No 131

Opposite

Alternate

WAYFARING TREE
(Viburnum lantana)

(from 129)

This species is more of a bush than a tree, but it may reach 6m and does its best to appear tree-like. It is unusual in having opposite leaves, which have small regular teeth. Their undersides and stalks are covered with downy hair.

The wayfaring tree is conspicuous in having small white flowers (6mm) growing in dense, rounded clusters up to 10cm in diameter. These become oval fruit, turning from green to red (when they are extremely noticeable) and eventually to black.

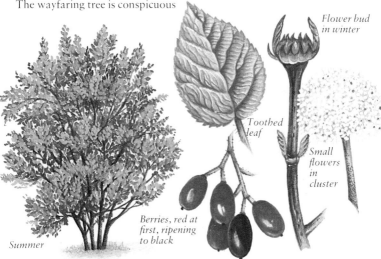

Flower bud in winter

Toothed leaf

Small flowers in cluster

Berries, red at first, ripening to black

Summer

131

Do the leaves have toothed margins?

(from 129)

Answer 'Yes' unless the margins of each leaf, though they may be wavy, are toothless.

Yes 132   No 137

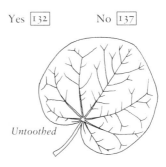

Toothed

Untoothed

Are the teeth prominent and regular?

Turn to 133 if the teeth on the leaf margins are both prominent and regular. Choose 134 if they are small, or vary considerably in size.

Yes 133   No 134

133
(from 132)

COMMON MULBERRY or Black Mulberry
(Morus nigra)

This species never grows to more than 10m. Its flowers are not conspicuous, but it can be recognized at once when in fruit. The berries, which look like raspberries, turn from green to red to purple-black, when they become soft and good to eat.

Its short trunk, which has a tendency to lean, is often blemished with burrs. The heart-shaped leaves (up to 15cm) have regular sharp teeth. Their hairs are rough to the touch on the upper surface, soft and downy below.

Almost always found in parks and gardens.

Summer

Ripe fruits

Toothed, heart-shaped leaves

Bark is scaled and rough on old trees

Do the leaves have pale undersides?

The remaining four species with heart-shaped leaves are the limes. Turn to 135 if the lower surfaces of the leaves are covered with silver-grey down, so that they are almost white in appearance. Otherwise turn to 136.

Yes | 135 | No | 136 |

| 135 | SILVER LIME
(*Tilia tomentosa*)

(from 134)

Of the four limes included, this species is at once distinguished by the downy grey hairs on the lower surfaces of its leaves (9–12cm), so that they are green above and silvery-grey below. The leaves' teeth are less regular but more prominent than the others'.

Otherwise the silver lime is similar to the other limes (see 136) in leaf-shape, fruit and flowers, and in its straight trunk, which is almost always single; but it grows less high, seldom exceeding 24m.

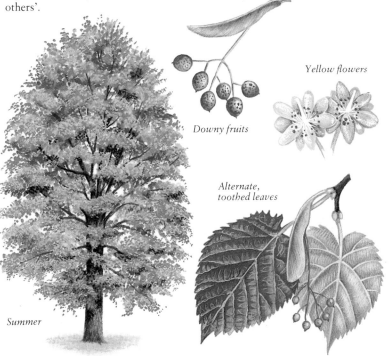

Downy fruits

Yellow flowers

Alternate, toothed leaves

Summer

COMMON LIME or European Lime
(*Tilia × europaea*)
SMALL-LEAVED LIME
(*Tilia cordata*)
LARGE-LEAVED LIME or Broad-leaved Lime
(*Tilia platyphyllos*)

These three limes are generally similar and it is best to consider them together. The common lime, which is indeed most often seen, is a hybrid of the other two.

Leaf size varies greatly, so may not be a certain guide, though the large-leaved lime does tend to have longer leaves (6–15cm) than the common (6–10cm) or the small-leaved (3–6cm). More distinctive are the noticeable hairs on the leaves of the large-leaved lime, especially on the upper surfaces. The other two species have completely hairless leaves, except perhaps for little tufts of hair on the undersides at the junctions of the veins. These are rust-coloured and often quite noticeable in the case of the small-leaved lime, whilst the common lime's are grey-white, sparser, and quite easy to miss.

The leaves of all three species have small regular teeth and are very definitely heart-shaped, though the bases of the common lime's may be less regular and indented than the others.

The little yellow flowers of these three handsome trees are quite similar, but those of the large-leaved lime almost always grow in threes. The small-leaved and common lime's are in clusters of 3–10. When they turn to fruit, only the small-leaved lime's (6mm) are completely hairless and unribbed. The common lime's (8mm) are faintly ribbed, and the large-leaved lime's (up to 10mm) are strongly ribbed.

It is the common lime whose trunk is sometimes, but by no means always, surrounded by a dense mass of upward-shooting suckers which may hide it for several metres. It reaches a greater height (50m) than any other tree in Britain excepting conifers. The two others seldom exceed 25–30m.

Winter

Hairy fruit, faintly ribbed

Leaf-like bract

COMMON LIME

Fragrant flower

Toothed, heart-shaped leaf

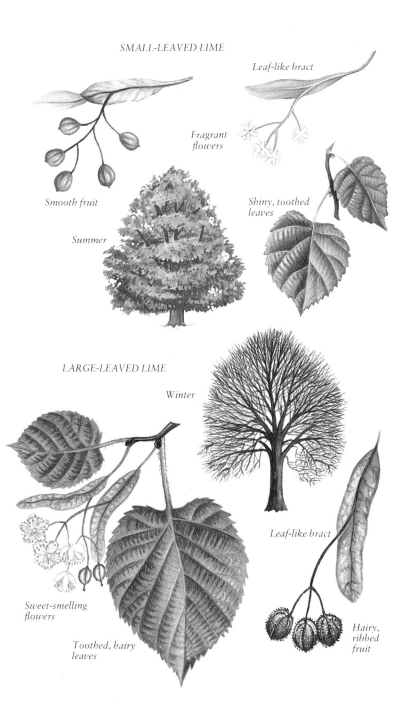

SMALL-LEAVED LIME

Leaf-like bract

Fragrant flowers

Smooth fruit

Shiny, toothed leaves

Summer

LARGE-LEAVED LIME

Winter

Leaf-like bract

Sweet-smelling flowers

Toothed, hairy leaves

Hairy, ribbed fruit

(from 131)

137 JUDAS TREE
(Cercis siliquastrum)

Pea-like flowers

If in bloom, this distinctive species is at once recognized by its clusters of pink flowers, shaped something like a pea's, which come out before the leaves. Some may sprout direct from the trunk itself. Its fruit is also pea-like, consisting of narrow pods (up to 12cm), which ripen from green to purple, then dark brown, and may stay on the tree all winter.

Pods ripen to purple

Alternate, rounded leaves

Alone among trees with heart-shaped foliage, its leaf-margins, which tend to be wavy, are completely smooth and toothless. The Judas tree never reaches a great height – seldom more than 10m – and usually branches out quickly to form a rounded, often lop-sided, crown.

Winter

138 Are there hairs on the surfaces of the leaves?
(from 121)

In choosing your answers, ignore any hairs that may be growing on the veins.

Upper side only 139
Both sides 140
Neither 141

ENGLISH ELM
(Ulmus procera)

Autumn leaf

This species, once among the commonest in the British Isles, has been the principal victim of Dutch elm disease, which is wiping it out in Britain and has now reached Ireland.

It is at once distinguished from other elms by the short, rough hairs, which feel like emery paper or stubble, on the upper surfaces of the leaves (up to 10cm). The undersides are hairless, except perhaps on the veins. The small crimson flowers are noticeable because they appear not later than March, long before the leaves. Indeed they have often developed into the single-winged seeds typical of elms before the foliage is fully out. The seeds (up to 12mm) turn from green to brown and usually fall in July.

This much-loved species almost always grows with a single straight stem and reaches 40m.

Alternate leaves with lop-sided bases

Flowers

Bark divided by long fissures

Summer

Winter

Fruit containing single seed

WYCH ELM
(Ulmus glabra)

(from 138)

The wych elm's dark green leaves have the same asymmetrical bases as the English elm's (see 139) but tend to be larger (up to 18cm) and more pointed. They are the only elm's to be hairy on both surfaces, with rough hairs above and softer hairs below.

The wych elm grows less tall (up to 30m) than the English elm, and its width is often greater than its height. This is because the trunk has a strong tendency to fork, with many sizeable branches spreading out into a dome-like crown.

The flowers and fruit of both species are similar, but the fruit of the wych elm tends to be larger (up to 15mm(. It is affected by Dutch elm disease, but less seriously than other species.

Hairy leaves with lop-sided bases

Summer

Flowers

Ripening seeds

Grey fissured bark

Winter

Single seed set in centre of fruit

Buds

SMOOTH-LEAVED ELM
(Ulmus carpinifolia)
DUTCH ELM
(Ulmus × hollandica)

There are many hybrids of the smooth-leaved elm, which often makes identification difficult, since a number of small variations may be noticed. But the Dutch elm is the only hybrid well enough known for inclusion in this book.

Both trees have flowers and fruit similar to other elms' (see 139 and 140), but their leaves are smooth and shiny, though borne on hairy or downy stalks. They may be distinguished from one another because the leaves of the smooth-leaved elm are almost or completely hairless. The under surfaces of the Dutch elm's have rough hairs on the veins and tufts of hair at the vein junctions (the axils). The smooth-leaved elm's leaves tend to be narrower. They are also usually smaller (6–8cm), though they may reach 12cm. The Dutch elm's are often 12–15cm.

Both trees grow to much the same maximum height (30m). They are so susceptible to the elm disease that their future is seriously threatened. (Dutch Elm illustrated on next page.)

Summer

Winged fruits

Shiny leaves with lop-sided bases

Tunnels made under the bark by the elm-bark beetle

SMOOTH-LEAVED ELM

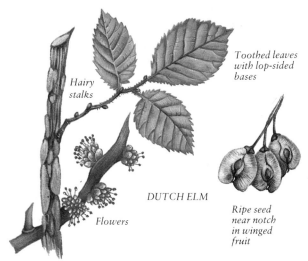

Hairy stalks

Toothed leaves with lop-sided bases

DUTCH ELM

Flowers

Ripe seed near notch in winged fruit

142   Are the leaves toothed?

(from 121)

Answer 'Yes' unless the margins of each leaf are wavy, and the teeth, if any, are extremely shallow.

Yes 143   No 152

Toothed

Untoothed

143   Is it a cherry?

(from 142)

When in bloom in early spring, the cherries may be distinguished from all other trees in this section by their delicate flowers, which are either pink or white. Later the fruit, if any, is always round and smooth; it turns from green to red, then in some cases to blue-black.

If not in flower or fruit, cherries are often distinguished by the unusual horizontal pattern of their bark. If in doubt, have a look at 144–146 before going on to 147 if necessary.

Yes 144   No 147

144
(from 114
and 143)

Does the bark have a strong, unpleasant smell?

Answer 'Yes' if the bark has a disagreeable smell of bitter almonds. Otherwise answer 'No'.

Yes 145   No 146

145
(from 144)

BIRD CHERRY
(Prunus padus)

The flowers of this species resemble those of other cherries, but are less showy, fragrant and much smaller (10−15mm). They hang downwards in long clusters. The fruit into which they develop is also smaller (8mm). Each cherry has its own stalk and ripens from green to red, but is so bitter that only birds eat it. The leaves (up to 12cm) are long and pointed with small, regular teeth.

The bird cherry is often shrub-like and seldom grows to any size, though it may reach 9m.

Toothed leaves

Flowers hang in long spikes

Ripe fruit

Unripe fruit

Horizontal patterned bark

Summer

146 WILD CHERRY or Gean or Mazzard
(Prunus avium)

(from 144)

The cherry is so popular that a large number of different ornamental species and varieties may be seen, almost always in parks and gardens. In the spring, they have very showy pink or white flowers, either single or double; they hardly every bear fruit. These are not covered in this book.

The wild cherry and the bird cherry (see 145) are the only ones to grow in woodland or hedgerows, and it is unusual to find them in gardens. The delicate white flowers of the wild cherry, which come out before the leaves, are a delight at Easter time. They are large (up to 35mm) and grow in bunches from woody bases or from the branch itself. They develop into round green fruit, later becoming red. The leaves are long and pointed with small forward-pointing teeth. They may turn red or yellow in autumn. The tree reaches 20m, and its wood is much prized as timber.

White flowers

Leaves are toothed and pointed

Ripe fruit

147 Do the leaves have prominent teeth?

(from 143)

Answer 'Yes' if there are prominent teeth along the margins of each leaf. Answer 'No' if any teeth are so small that they are barely visible.

Yes 148   No 151

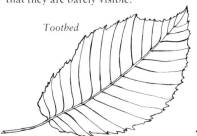

Toothed

Untoothed

148 Is the trunk fluted?

(from 147)

Choose 149 if the lower trunk,
despite its smooth grey bark, is
irregularly fluted, often deeply. Turn
to 150 if the trunk, like that of most
trees, tends to be cylindrical.

Yes 149   No 150

149 HORNBEAM
(Carpinus betulus)

(from 148)

The leaves of the hornbeam are often
mistaken for the beech's (see 152),
but in fact are quite different. Apart
from having irregular teeth instead of
a wavy, toothless margin, they have
extremely prominent, deeply
impressed veins, in parallel pairs,
which are clearly noticeable even at
some distance.

Each tree carries catkins of both
sexes, which appear in March,
usually with the leaves. The male

flowers are much the more
conspicuous, up to 5cm in length,
greenish-yellow and soon drooping
downward. But the females develop
into even more noticeable fruit in
hanging clusters of 3-lobed bracts,
like small pointed leaves, each with a
small nut. These, like the foliage,
turn from green to brown.

Hornbeam timber is very hard and
has many uses. The tree reaches a
height of 30m.

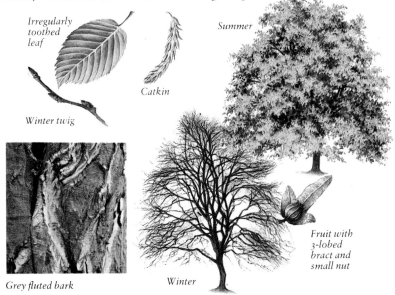

Irregularly toothed leaf

Catkin

Winter twig

Summer

Fruit with 3-lobed bract and small nut

Grey fluted bark

Winter

SILVER BIRCH
(Betula pendula)
GREY ALDER
(Aldus incana)

These two members of the birch family are taken together because their leaves vary in shape and may be confusingly similar. In both cases they are always irregularly toothed and come to a definite point. Those of the silver birch are usually more or less straight-based, making them roughly triangular, but sometimes their bases are more rounded, when they are like the grey alder's. The sure distinction is that the latter's, but not the former's, have fine hairs on the underside.

When mature, the better-known silver birch is instantly recognized by its pure white bark, often pock-marked with black. But this is not the case with young trees, whose bark is brown with a distinctive rust-coloured tinge, later pinkish-white. In any case, it is very different from the grey alder's, which is yellowish-grey.

The grey alder grows naturally beside rivers, but is widely used for the reclamation of wasteland, whether wet or dry. It may be recognized in winter because most of its round fruit, originally green but now blackened, does not fall from the tree. The dangling male catkins of the silver birch are conspicuous in spring. The females, at first green and erect, later hang downward; their winged seeds fall in winter.

The silver birch is at home in dry ground and is often planted in city streets. Usually neither species reaches a great height (not more than 15m), but occasional specimens may attain 24–30m.

Winter

Female catkins

Male catkin

Irregularly toothed leaves

Yellow autumn leaf

Winged seed

Fruiting catkin

SILVER BIRCH

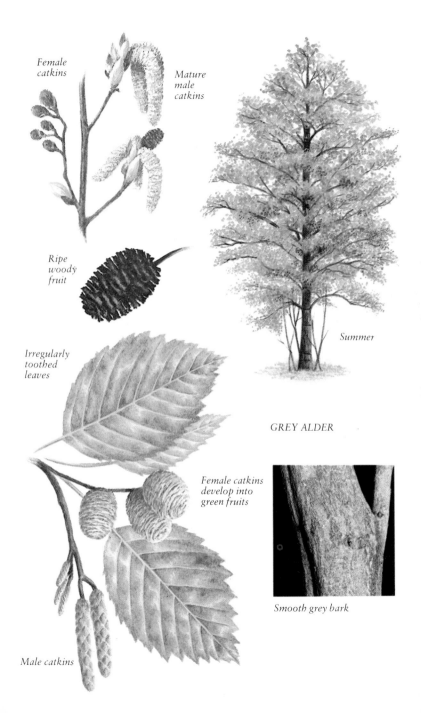

Female catkins

Mature male catkins

Ripe woody fruit

Irregularly toothed leaves

GREY ALDER

Female catkins develop into green fruits

Male catkins

Smooth grey bark

BLACK POPLAR
(Populus nigra var *betulifolia)*
SEROTINA POPLAR or Black Italian Poplar
(Populus nigra 'Serotina')

The true black poplar *(Populus nigra)* is seldom seen in Britain. Many varieties and hybrids have been developed, three of which are widely enough planted for inclusion in this book: the Lombardy poplar (see 126) and these two, which it is best to consider together.

Their leaves are hairless, except those of the *betulifolia* variety when they first come out. Otherwise they are quite hard to tell apart, except that the serotina's are at first almost copper-coloured. They are rather variable in shape, but in both cases come to a very distinct point and have rounded sides with hardly noticeable teeth.

The *betulifolia* variety, usually known simply as 'black poplar', may be distinguished by the large, rounded burrs that often protrude from its trunk. These should not be confused with the unsightly black cankers that may disfigure the serotina, which is much the more widely planted.

The serotina's trunk is usually straight and does not often divide. The tree grows extremely quickly and may reach 40m. The black poplar does not exceed 30m. Its trunk is frequently divided and its much heavier branches are far less regular.

BLACK POPLAR

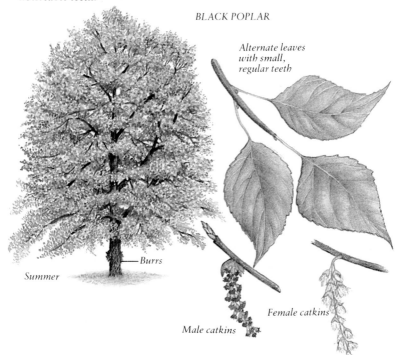

*Alternate leaves
with small,
regular teeth*

Burrs

Summer

Male catkins

Female catkins

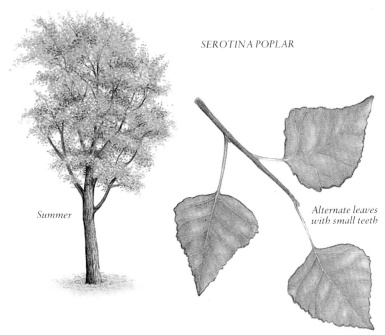

SEROTINA POPLAR

Summer

Alternate leaves with small teeth

152

(from 142)

COMMON BEECH or European Beech
(Fagus sylvatica)

Leaves alternate with wavy margins

Female flowers

Male flowers

COMMON BEECH
(see also on next page)

The common beech is one of the best-known and noblest trees, sometimes exceeding 40m in height. It is always recognizable by its smooth grey bark, which never grows fissured with age.

The male flowers grow in small yellow clusters from long stalks. The female are inconspicuous, but develop into the well-known fruit, beech mast, which is green and soft at first, but later turns brown and woody. Each fruit splits into four segments to release the two triangular nuts.

Beech leaves are oval with wavy margins. They may reach 10cm in length but are usually shorter, with 6–8 pairs of parallel veins. When

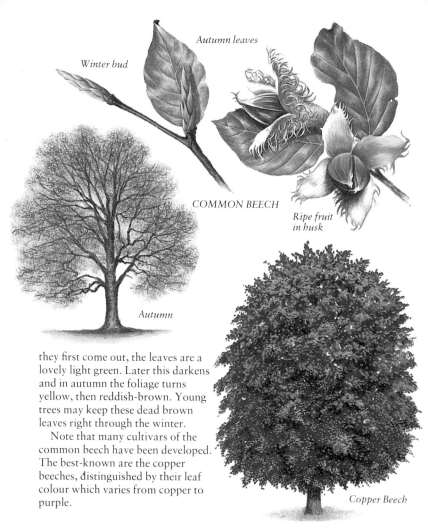

Winter bud

Autumn leaves

COMMON BEECH

Ripe fruit in husk

Autumn

Copper Beech

they first come out, the leaves are a lovely light green. Later this darkens and in autumn the foliage turns yellow, then reddish-brown. Young trees may keep these dead brown leaves right through the winter.

Note that many cultivars of the common beech have been developed. The best-known are the copper beeches, distinguished by their leaf colour which varies from copper to purple.

153 · What type are the compound leaves?

(from 67)

Compound leaves are of three distinct kinds. Occasionally they are *trifoliate*, which means they have three short-stalked leaflets (not more), all much the same size, growing from the same point on the leaf stalk.

If they are *palmate*, they have 5–7 leaflets which radiate like a fan. The middle one is the largest, the others progressively smaller on either side of it.

Pinnate leaves are quite different. Their leaflets grow from a central

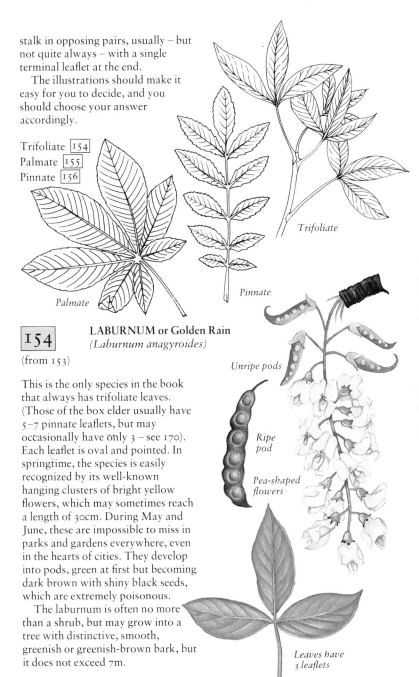

stalk in opposing pairs, usually – but not quite always – with a single terminal leaflet at the end.

The illustrations should make it easy for you to decide, and you should choose your answer accordingly.

Trifoliate ⟨154⟩
Palmate ⟨155⟩
Pinnate ⟨156⟩

Palmate

Trifoliate

Pinnate

⟨154⟩ **LABURNUM or Golden Rain**
(Laburnum anagyroides)

(from 153)

This is the only species in the book that always has trifoliate leaves. (Those of the box elder usually have 5–7 pinnate leaflets, but may occasionally have only 3 – see 170). Each leaflet is oval and pointed. In springtime, the species is easily recognized by its well-known hanging clusters of bright yellow flowers, which may sometimes reach a length of 30cm. During May and June, these are impossible to miss in parks and gardens everywhere, even in the hearts of cities. They develop into pods, green at first but becoming dark brown with shiny black seeds, which are extremely poisonous.

The laburnum is often no more than a shrub, but may grow into a tree with distinctive, smooth, greenish or greenish-brown bark, but it does not exceed 7m.

Unripe pods

Ripe pod

Pea-shaped flowers

Leaves have 3 leaflets

155

(from 153)

HORSE CHESTNUT
(*Aesculus hippocastanum*)
RED HORSE CHESTNUT
(*Aesculus × carnea*)

The horse chestnut is one of the best-known species, with its sticky brown buds, its magnificent white 'candles', its very large leaves (up to 25cm) with 5–7 stalkless leaflets, and its rather spiny, rounded green fruit, each holding 1–3 nuts – the much-prized 'conkers'.

The red horse chestnut, usually seen in parks and gardens, is a hybrid between the horse chestnut and an American species, the red buckeye. Apart from its pinkish-red 'candles', which are usually smaller with less densely packed flowers, it is generally similar. But the buds are not sticky, the fruit is usually not spiny and the nuts are too small for conkers. It seldom exceeds 20m – half the maximum height of the other.

Both trees usually have an undivided trunk and a fine spreading crown.

Flowers

Bud becomes sticky in spring

Open fruit showing conker

HORSE CHESTNUT

RED HORSE CHESTNUT

Leaves have 5–7 leaflets

Spike of flowers

Winter

156

(from 153)

Are the leaflets toothed?

Answer 'Yes' if the leaflets have toothed margins. Answer 'No' if they do not have teeth (except perhaps one or two large ones at the leaflet's base), though they may have rounded lobes.

Yes 157   No 164

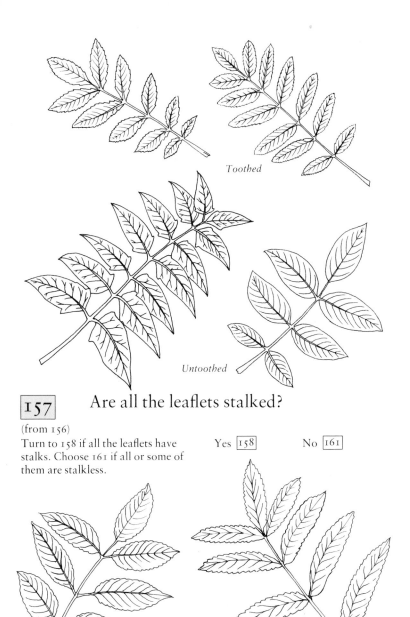

Toothed

Untoothed

Are all the leaflets stalked?

(from 156)
Turn to 158 if all the leaflets have
stalks. Choose 161 if all or some of
them are stalkless.

Yes 158   No 161

Leaflets stalked

Leaflets unstalked

158
(from 157)

Do the leaves have a strong, pungent smell?

Answer 'Yes' if the leaves, when crushed, have a noticeable odour. Otherwise answer 'No'.

Yes 159   No 160

159
(from 158)

ELDER or Bourtree
(Sambucus nigra)

The elder's small white flowers grow in rather flat-topped, erect umbels. When they become berries, they droop downward and turn from green to red to black. The 5–7 leaflets have many pointed regular teeth. They are oval in shape but pointed and have noticeable stalks.

The elder is often shrub-like, but on suitable ground, often near houses, it can reach 9m, though its grey-brown, ridged trunk may divide early. The flowers and ripe fruit are both used for making wine.

Fragrant flowers in erect clusters

Leaf has 5–7 leaflets

Ripe berries

Summer

(from 158)

160 MANNA ASH or Flowering Ash
(Fraxinus ornus)

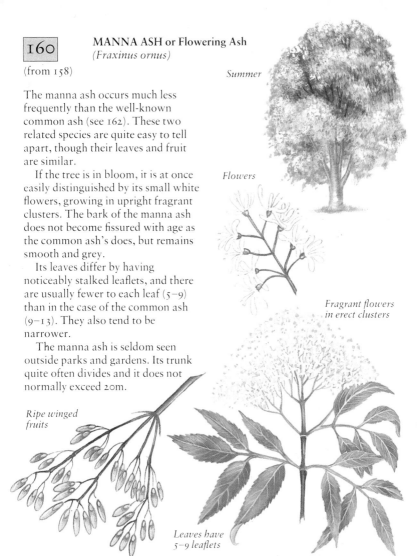

Summer

The manna ash occurs much less frequently than the well-known common ash (see 162). These two related species are quite easy to tell apart, though their leaves and fruit are similar.

If the tree is in bloom, it is at once easily distinguished by its small white flowers, growing in upright fragrant clusters. The bark of the manna ash does not become fissured with age as the common ash's does, but remains smooth and grey.

Its leaves differ by having noticeably stalked leaflets, and there are usually fewer to each leaf (5–9) than in the case of the common ash (9–13). They also tend to be narrower.

The manna ash is seldom seen outside parks and gardens. Its trunk quite often divides and it does not normally exceed 20m.

Flowers

Fragrant flowers in erect clusters

Ripe winged fruits

Leaves have 5–9 leaflets

161 Are its leaves opposite?

(from 157)

The leaflets, in all cases, grow in opposite pairs along their mid-rib. Answer 'Yes' if the leaves, too, grow in opposite pairs from their twigs. Answer 'No' if they are alternate.

Yes 162   No 163

COMMON ASH or European Ash
(Fraxinus excelsior)

(from 161)

The common ash is one of our best known trees. It regenerates naturally on any suitable ground and thrives almost everywhere, growing into a fine forest tree up to 40m in height. At first its bark is smooth and silver-grey. This colour darkens with age and vertical fissures begin to appear, which become increasingly conspicuous.

Small purple flowers are noticeable in the early spring because they appear before the leaves, which are among the last to come out. At this season its sooty black buds are also unmistakable. The leaflets of the common ash are stalkless, unlike those of the manna ash (see 160). There are usually 9–13 to each leaf.

The fruits of both species are single-winged, hanging in dense clusters. They turn from green to brown and are often to be seen long after all the leaves have fallen. The common ash almost always grows with a straight, cylindrical trunk, undivided for most of its length. Its very hard timber has many important uses and also makes excellent firewood.

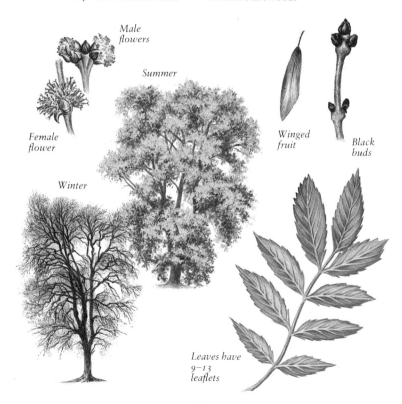

Male flowers

Summer

Female flower

Winged fruit

Black buds

Winter

Leaves have 9–13 leaflets

163

ROWAN or Mountain Ash
(Sorbus acuparia)
TRUE SERVICE TREE
(Sorbus domestica)

(from 161)

Both these related species bear clusters of small white flowers. The rowan's are distinguished by their strong smell; they are more densely packed and flatter-topped. The fruits are even more distinctive. The rowan has round berries (up to 8mm), hanging in large bunches. Briefly green, they turn bright scarlet and are exceedingly conspicuous. Those of the true service tree are pear-shaped, less numerous, less brightly coloured, and much larger (up to 3cm). The leaves of both are similar, with stalkless toothed leaflets of about the same length (up to 20cm). The true service tree may have rather more leaflets to a leaf (13–21) than the rowan (11–15).

When not in fruit or flower, the bark is the most distinctive feature. The rowan's is smooth and shiny, grey becoming grey-brown. The service tree's is rough and reddish-brown, with rectangular fissures in the case of older treees. The rowan is more graceful with lighter branches. Both species reach 15–20m.

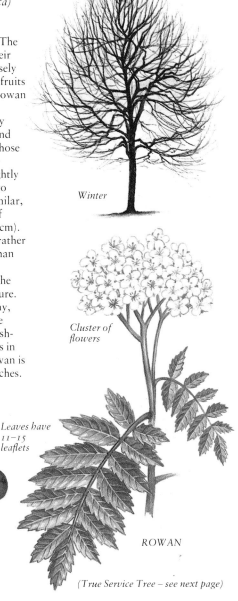

Winter

Cluster of flowers

Leaves have 11–15 leaflets

Ripe berries

ROWAN

(True Service Tree – see next page)

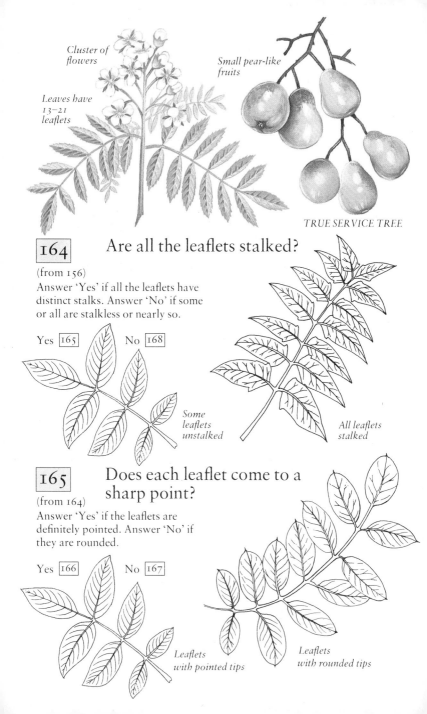

Cluster of flowers

Leaves have 13–21 leaflets

Small pear-like fruits

TRUE SERVICE TREE

164 Are all the leaflets stalked?

(from 156)

Answer 'Yes' if all the leaflets have distinct stalks. Answer 'No' if some or all are stalkless or nearly so.

Yes 165   No 168

Some leaflets unstalked

All leaflets stalked

165 Does each leaflet come to a sharp point?

(from 164)

Answer 'Yes' if the leaflets are definitely pointed. Answer 'No' if they are rounded.

Yes 166   No 167

Leaflets with pointed tips

Leaflets with rounded tips

TREE OF HEAVEN
(Ailanthus altissima)

(from 165)

This handsome Chinese tree is well able to withstand pollution and is therefore often planted for ornament in city parks and streets.

Its leaves always have at least 11 stalked leaflets, generally far more, growing in pairs with or without a terminal leaflet. They are very sharply pointed and are unusual in having 1–4 large teeth at the base of each – usually just a pair. The male and female flowers, almost always on separate trees, are rather similar, both being greenish-white in clusters. The latter develop into hanging, winged fruit, up to 4cm long, with one seed in each wing. They turn from green to brown.

The bark is usually grey and very smooth, something like a beech's, but it may darken and develop small vertical cracks as the tree grows older. A height of 25m may be attained.

Winter

Ripe winged fruits

Flowers

Leaves with stalked leaflets

FALSE ACACIA or Robinia or Locust Tree or Black Locust
(Robinia pseudoacacia)

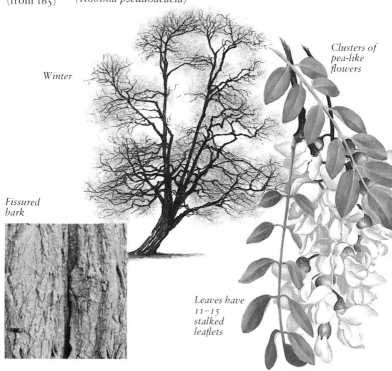

Winter

Clusters of pea-like flowers

Fissured bark

Leaves have 11–15 stalked leaflets

This decorative species has oval, hairless leaflets, with rounded ends and a small spine protruding from each tip. There are usually 11–15 to each leaf, which may reach 20cm in length. It has fragrant white flowers, rather like a pea's, which come out in June and hang in dangling clusters. These later become pods, 5–10cm long, which turn from green to brown in autumn and often stay on the tree all winter. They hold black, kidney-shaped seeds.

Like so many trees, its bark is smooth at first, but with age becomes deeply fissured. It is almost always grown ornamentally in parks and gardens, reaching a height of 20m.

168
(from 164)

Are there fewer than ten leaflets?

Choose 169 if each compound leaf has 5–9 leaflets. Turn to 172 if there are at least 11 and maybe many more.

Yes 169   No 172

Are the leaf margins lobed?

(from 168)

Answer 'Yes' if the margins have unmistakable lobes. Answer 'No' if they have neither lobes nor teeth.

Yes 170   No 171

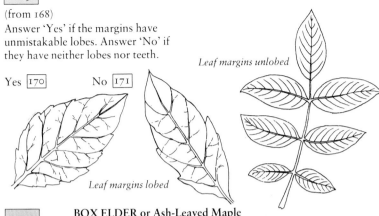

Leaf margins unlobed

Leaf margins lobed

170

BOX ELDER or Ash-Leaved Maple
(Acer negundo)

(from 169)

This small tree is in fact a maple, though its leaves are nothing like any other's. They rather resemble an elder's, but their 5–7 leaflets (occasionally 3) have lobes rather than teeth.

Box elders are either male or female. The male flowers are reddish and grow in hanging clusters. The females are less conspicuous; they develop into the winged seeds typical of maples, but their tips are unusual in curving inwards. The box elder grows quickly but is short-lived. It is often bush-like but may reach 14m.

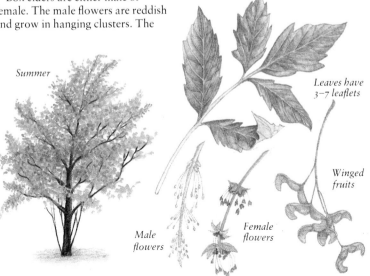

Summer

Leaves have 3–7 leaflets

Winged fruits

Male flowers

Female flowers

COMMON WALNUT or English Walnut
(Juglans regia)

(from 169)

The walnut is one of the last trees to come into leaf – seldom before the second half of May. At first its foliage is yellow-brown, soon becoming green.

Each leaf usually has 7–9 leaflets, occasionally 5, with no stalks or very short ones. Their margins are toothless or nearly so. The terminal leaflet is the largest; each pair then grows progressively smaller. The male flowers are dangling catkins (5–15cm), which appear just before the leaves. The females are incon-spicuous. The grey bark is smooth in young trees, but becomes fissured with age.

Walnuts are greatly prized, not only for their well-known nuts (which grow inside a round green fruit) but even more – eventually – for their timber, which is extremely valuable if suitable for veneering. This handsome species grows into a magnificent tree with a spreading crown and a stout, straight trunk. It reaches a height of 30m.

Summer

Leaf usually has 7–9 leaflets

Unripe fruit

Male catkin

Winter

Open fruit shows an edible walnut

HONEY LOCUST
(Gleditsia triacanthos)

(from 168)

The leaves of the honey locust have 14–36 unstalked leaflets, narrower than those of the preceding species, with barely visible teeth. Usually, but not quite always, there is no terminal leaflet. Sometimes the leaves are bipinnate: each leaf has pinnate leaflets, which themselves have pinnate leaflets.

Fragrant male and female flowers grow in separate clusters on the same tree. The females are less conspicuous than the males, which are greenish-yellow catkins (about 5cm). The fruit is extremely noticeable, but only prolific in hot summers. It consists of very long, narrow pods (25–45cm), often twisting, which turn from green to brown as they ripen. Also unmistakable are the clumps of spiny thorns that may protrude at intervals from the bark, which is usually ridged and scaly. A height of 18m may be attained.

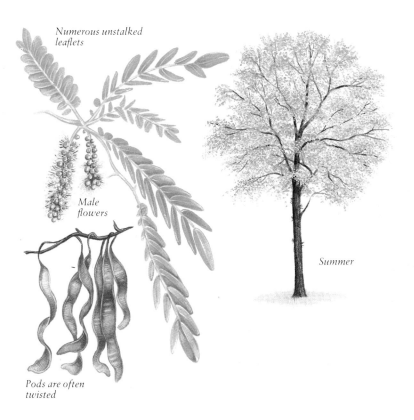

Numerous unstalked leaflets

Male flowers

Summer

Pods are often twisted

Key

When you find you no longer need the help of detailed Questions, it will become more convenient to use this abbreviated key, which should lead you much more quickly towards your Answer.

TREES WITH NEEDLE-LIKE LEAVES

Leaves growing singly
{
Leaves all in much the same plane
{
Deciduous 5
Evergreen 6
}

Leaves in several different planes
{
Leaves with "pegs" 12
Leaves in whorls of 3 15
Neither of above 16
}

Leaves not growing singly
{
Leaves in pairs from same base
{
Leaves less than 10cm 31
Leaves about 15cm 34
Leaves up to 25cm 35
}

Leaves in threes from same base 36

Leaves in fives from same base
{
Delicate blue needles 37
Stiff green needles 38
}

Leaves in tufts of ten or more
{
Deciduous 41
Evergreen 42
}

TREES WITH SCALE-LIKE LEAVES

Fruit berry-like 45

Fruit cone-like ....
{
Cones 10mm or less
{
Cones spherical 48
Cones elongated 49
}

Cones over 20mm 50
}

BROAD-LEAVED TREES (all others)

(i) Evergreen

Grey undersides 53

Green undersides
{
Leaves narrow ....
{
Aromatic 56
Not aromatic 57
}

Leaves not narrow ....
{
Leaves less than 4cm 61
Leaves 6–10cm 64
}
}

(ii) Deciduous – simple leaves

(iii) Deciduous – compound leaves

A hornbeam on the author's land at Killegar, with leaves and flowers coming out together in April.

Index and Checklist

Use the boxes to mark with an 'X' each new species as you see it. There are spare boxes at the end for you to insert rare species that are not included in the book.

ENGLISH NAMES

☐ . . . .
☐ . . . .
☐ . . . .
☐ . . . .
☐ . . . .
☐ . . . .
☐ . . . .

SCIENTIFIC NAMES

Notes